Windows 3.0

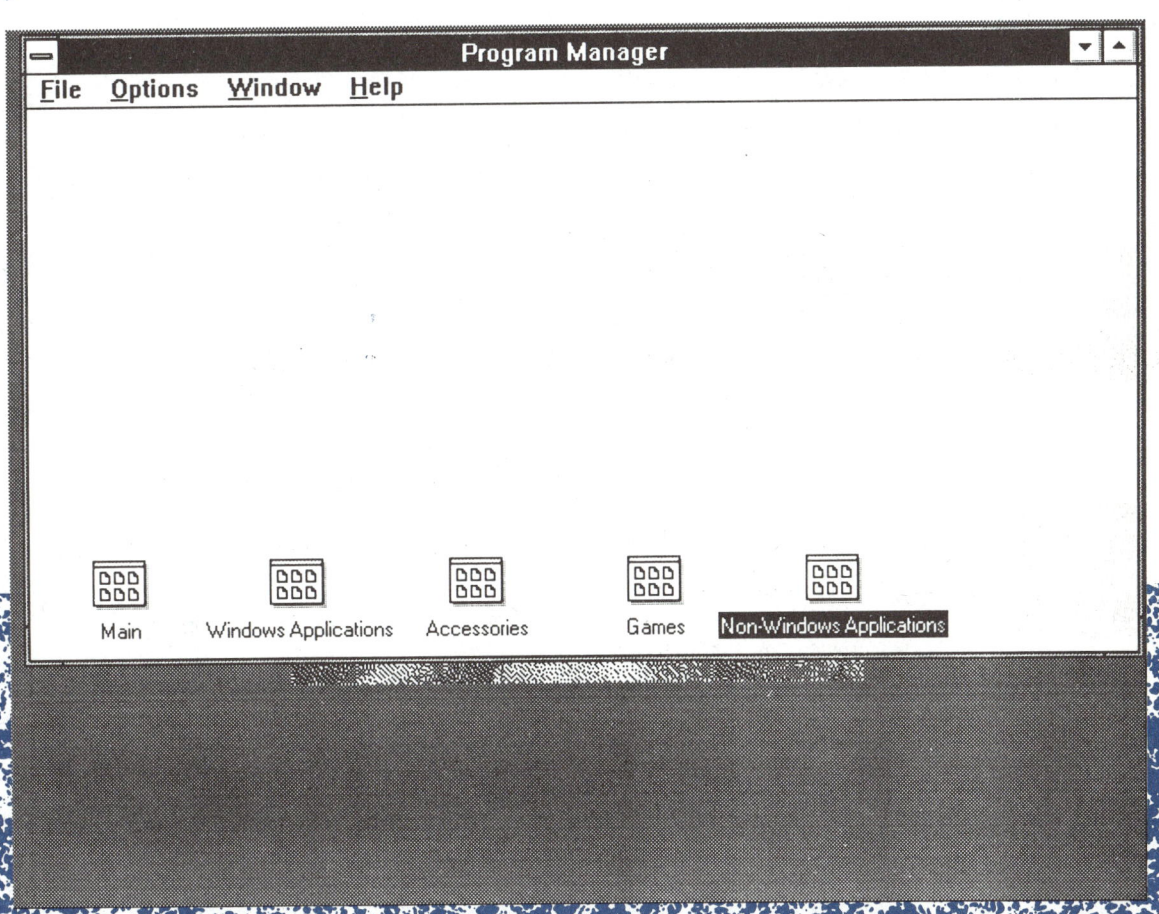

Computer users are not all alike.
Neither are SYBEX books.

We know our customers have a variety of needs. They've told us so. And because we've listened, we've developed several distinct types of books to meet the needs of each of our customers. What are you looking for in computer help?

If you're looking for the basics, try the **ABC's** series. You'll find short, unintimidating tutorials and helpful illustrations. For a more visual approach, select **Teach Yourself**, featuring screen-by-screen illustrations of how to use your latest software purchase.

Mastering and **Understanding** titles offer you a step-by-step introduction, plus an in-depth examination of intermediate-level features, to use as you progress.

Our **Up & Running** series is designed for computer-literate consumers who want a no-nonsense overview of new programs. Just 20 basic lessons, and you're on your way.

We also publish two types of reference books. Our **Instant References** provide quick access to each of a program's commands and functions. SYBEX **Encyclopedias** provide a *comprehensive reference* and explanation of all of the commands, features and functions of the subject software.

Sometimes a subject requires a special treatment that our standard series doesn't provide. So you'll find we have titles like **Advanced Techniques, Handbooks, Tips & Tricks**, and others that are specifically tailored to satisfy a unique need.

We carefully select our authors for their in-depth understanding of the software they're writing about, as well as their ability to write clearly and communicate effectively. Each manuscript is thoroughly reviewed by our technical staff to ensure its complete accuracy. Our production department makes sure it's easy to use. All of this adds up to the highest quality books available, consistently appearing on best-seller charts worldwide.

You'll find SYBEX publishes a variety of books on every popular software package. Looking for computer help? Help Yourself to SYBEX.

For a complete catalog of our publications:

SYBEX Inc.
2021 Challenger Drive, Alameda, CA 94501
Tel: (415) 523-8233/(800) 227-2346 Telex: 336311
SYBEX Fax: (415) 523-2373

SYBEX is committed to using natural resources wisely to preserve and improve our environment. As a leader in the computer book publishing industry, we are aware that over 40% of America's solid waste is paper. This is why we have been printing the text of books like this one on recycled paper since 1982.

This year our use of recycled paper will result in the saving of more than 15,300 trees. We will lower air pollution effluents by 54,000 pounds, save 6,300,000 gallons of water, and reduce landfill by 2,700 cubic yards.

In choosing a SYBEX book you are not only making a choice for the best in skills and information, you are also choosing to enhance the quality of life for all of us.

The ABC's of IBM PCs and Compatibles

The ABC's of IBM® PCs and Compatibles

Third Edition

Joan Lasselle and Carol Ramsay

SYBEX®

San Francisco•Paris•Düsseldorf•Soest

Acquisitions Editor: Dianne King
Developmental Editor: James A. Compton
Editor: Kenyon Brown
Technical Editor: Daniel Tauber
Production Editor: Carolina Montilla
Word Processors: Ann Dunn, Susan Trybull
Book Designer: Suzanne Albertson
Chapter Art and Layout: Lucie Živny
Technical Art: Delia Brown
Screen Graphics: Cuong Le
Typesetter: Stephanie Hollier
Proofreaders: Lisa Haden, Hilda van Genderen
Indexer: Julie Kawabata
Cover Designer: Thomas Ingalls + Associates
Cover Photographer: Mark Johann

SYBEX is a registered trademark of SYBEX, Inc.

TRADEMARKS: SYBEX has attempted throughout this book to distinguish proprietary trademarks from descriptive terms by following the capitalization style used by the manufacturer.

SYBEX is not affiliated with any manufacturer.

Every effort has been made to supply complete and accurate information. However, SYBEX assumes no responsibility for its use, nor for any infringement of the intellectual property rights of third parties which would result from such use.

First edition copyright ©1984 SYBEX Inc.

Second edition copyright ©1988 SYBEX Inc.

Copyright ©1991 SYBEX Inc., 2021 Challenger Drive, Alameda, CA 94501. World rights reserved. No part of this publication may be stored in a retrieval system, transmitted, or reproduced in any way, including but not limited to photocopy, photograph, magnetic or other record, without the prior agreement and written permission of the publisher.

Library of Congress Card Number: 91-65438
ISBN: 0-89588-812-2

Manufactured in the United States of America
10 9 8 7 6 5 4 3 2 1

Acknowledgments

We would like to thank our staff for making this new edition of *The ABC's of IBM PCs and Compatibles* possible. Vince Leone and Becky Levine updated the previous edition and wrote the chapters on the DOS 5 Shell, Windows, and using applications.

We would also like to thank the editor, Kenyon Brown, and the rest of the SYBEX staff for their contributions and hard work.

Contents at a Glance

Introduction		xix
PART I: AN INTRODUCTION TO YOUR PC	**1**	
1 Anatomy of Your PC		2
2 Beginning with the Basics		18
PART II: USING THE DOS COMMAND LINE	**35**	
3 Commands for Your PC		36
4 All about Diskettes		46
5 Building a Filing System		64
PART III: USING OPERATING ENVIRONMENTS	**93**	
6 Using the DOS 5 Shell		94
7 Windows 3.0 Work Session		116
PART IV: USING APPLICATIONS	**139**	
8 Computer Applications: Tools for Your PC		140
9 Application Work Sessions		148
PART V: BEYOND THE BASICS	**173**	
10 Bells and Whistles: Optional Components		174
11 Checklists: If Something Goes Wrong		182
APPENDIXES		
A Putting It All Together		188
B Glossary		196
C Resources		204
Index		**215**

*T*able of Contents

Introduction   xix

**PART I
AN INTRODUCTION TO YOUR PC**   1

1   Anatomy of Your PC   2

Hardware   3
    The System Unit   3
    The Hard Disk Drive   4
    The Keyboard   5
    The Diskette Drive   7
    The Display   7
    The Mouse   8
Software   10
    The Disk Operating System   10
    Operating Environments   10
    Application Programs   11
Review   15

2   Beginning with the Basics   18

Turning on Your PC   19
Setting the Date and Time   20
    The Cursor   21
    Correcting Mistakes   21
    Entering What You Have Typed   22

The DOS Prompt	23
Using the Diskette Drive	23
Inserting a Diskette	23
Changing the Current Drive	25
The Shift Keys	25
Removing a Diskette	26
Getting Familiar with the Keyboard	27
The Numeric Keypad and the Arrow Keys	27
The Function Keys	28
The Ctrl Key	28
The Esc Key	29
Resetting Your PC	30
Turning Off Your PC	31
Review	32

PART II
USING THE DOS COMMAND LINE   35

3   Commands for Your PC   36

Typing Commands	37
Freezing the Display	39
Upper- and Lowercase	41
The Caps Lock Key	41
Canceling a Command	42
Choosing from Menus	43
Using the Function Keys	44
Review	44

4 All about Diskettes — 46

Rules for Handling Diskettes	49
Labeling Diskettes	50
Storing Diskettes	52
Copying Diskettes	52
The DISKCOPY Command	53
Write-Protecting Diskettes	55
5¼-inch Diskettes	55
3½-inch Diskettes	55
Formatting a Diskette	56
Checking Diskette Storage Space	58
The CHKDSK Command	59
Cleaning Diskette Drives	61
Review	61

5 Building a Filing System — 64

Designing Your Filing System	66
Assigning Directory Names	67
Rules for Directory Names	67
Creating a Directory	68
Changing the Current Directory	69
Using Path Names for Directories	71
Removing a Directory	72
Assigning File Names	73
Rules for File Names	73
Using Path Names for Files	75
Wild Card Characters	76
Copying Files	77
Making a Copy on Another Disk	77

Making a Copy in Another Directory	79
Making a Copy in the Same Directory	80
Renaming a File	80
Erasing or Deleting a File	81
Backing Up Your File System	83
Backup Methods	83
Using the Backup Command	84
Using the RESTORE Command	86
Review	87

PART III
USING OPERATING ENVIRONMENTS   93

6   Using the DOS 5 Shell   94

Loading the Shell	96
The DOS Shell	96
Executing Commands in the DOS Shell	98
Using the Mouse with Menus	98
Using the Keyboard with Menus	99
Changing the View in the DOS Shell	99
Changing the View with the Mouse	100
Changing the View with the Keyboard	101
Working with the Directory Tree	101
Selecting a Directory	102
Changing the Directory Tree Display	102
Working with the File Area	104
Sorting Files	104
Other Sorting Options	105
Creating a File	106

Selecting Files	107
Copying a File to Another Directory	108
Renaming a File	109
Moving a File	110
Deleting a File	111
Running Executable Files	111
Working with the Program Area	112
Using the Task Swapper	113
Review	115

7 Windows 3.0 Work Session 116

Running Windows on a 386 Computer	118
Loading Windows	118
The Program Manager Window	119
Opening an Application Window	120
Using the Mouse to Open Write	121
Using the Keyboard	122
Elements of an Application Window	123
Working with Menus	123
Using the Mouse	124
Using the Keyboard	124
Working with a Single Window	125
Saving a Document	126
Changing the Size of a Window	127
Scrolling through a Window	128
Working with Two or More Windows	129
Starting in Cardfile	131
Working in Cardfile	132
Arranging Windows on the Desktop	132
Transferring Information between Windows	134

Changing the Active Window	135
Changing the Window with Switch To	135
Review	137

PART IV
USING APPLICATIONS 139

8 Computer Applications: Tools for Your PC 140

Installing an Application	142
Making a Backup Copy	142
Loading an Application Program	143
Using an Application Program	144
Entering and Saving Information	144
Retrieving the Information	145
Revising the Information	145
Printing the Information	146
Review	146

9 Application Work Sessions 148

WordPerfect 5.1 Work Session	149
Loading WordPerfect	150
The WordPerfect Screen	150
WordPerfect Commands	150
Entering Text	152
Moving the Cursor	153
Inserting Text	153
Deleting Text	154

Typing over Text	156
Saving the Document	157
Printing the Document	158
Clearing the Screen	159
Leaving WordPerfect	159
Listing the Files	160
Lotus 1-2-3 Work Session	160
Loading 1-2-3	161
The 1-2-3 Worksheet	161
Creating a Report	164
Moving the Cell Pointer	165
Entering Labels	165
Entering Values (Numbers)	166
Entering a Formula	167
Using Menus	167
Saving Your Report	169
Printing Your Report	169
Leaving 1-2-3	170
Review	171

PART V
BEYOND THE BASICS — 173

10 Bells and Whistles: Optional Components — 174

Extra Disk Drives	176
Printers	176
Additional Memory	177

Color and Graphics Displays	178
Game Control Adapters	178
Plotters	179
Communications Adapters	179

11 Checklists: If Something Goes Wrong — 182

Your Checklist	184
PC Checklist	185
Service	185

APPENDIXES — 188

A Putting It All Together — 188

Choosing a Location	190
Unpacking the System Unit	190
Connecting the Keyboard	191
Connecting the Display	192
Connecting the Power Cord	193
Adjusting the Keyboard	194

B Glossary — 196

C Resources — 204

Magazines	205
Information Services	208
Public Information Services	208

Database Vendors	210
Electronic Mail Services	215

Index *215*

Introduction

Whether you have just purchased an IBM or IBM-compatible personal computer to use at home or whether you found one on your desk when you arrived at work this morning, this book is for you, the PC user.

We assume that you have little or no experience with PCs (or any other computer), and that you are not going to write your own programs—at least, not right away. Rather, you will be using purchased programs, called applications, such as Lotus 1-2-3 or Word-Perfect. You are anxious to learn the basics and put your PC to work. But where do you start?

This book is designed to get you started. Because you learn best by doing, we include exercises so that you can practice on your own PC as we go along. We will have you loading, entering, saving, and retrieving in no time. Here are the things we are going to talk about:

Chapter 1 introduces you to the parts of your PC: the hardware and the software. It describes the function of each component and discusses the different kinds of software applications you will probably be using.

Chapter 2 gets you started. You turn on the PC, load the operating system, set the date and time, and learn how to use the keyboard and diskette drive.

Chapter 3 shows you how to communicate with your PC using simple commands, menu selections, and function keys.

Chapter 4 tells you all about using diskettes. It includes proper handling, storage, labeling, and protection of diskettes. In addition, you will learn how to format and copy them.

Chapter 5 tells you how to organize the files on your hard disk. You learn how to create and use directories, how to name, list, copy, rename and delete files, and how to back up the important information in your system.

Chapter 6 contains instructions and exercises for using the DOS 5 Shell, the graphical interface that is provided with version 5 of DOS.

Chapter 7 introduces you to Microsoft Windows. This work session gets you started in using this popular operating environment.

Chapter 8 discusses application programs in general.

Chapter 9 introduces you to WordPerfect and Lotus 1-2-3. Two short work sessions give you a feel for word processing and spreadsheets.

Chapter 10 describes additional components that you can add to your PC to perform special functions such as printing, graphics, and communications.

Chapter 11 provides you with a checklist for problem-solving if things do not go as planned.

In addition, there are three appendices. One tells you how to unpack and set up your PC, another provides you with a glossary of terms, and the final one offers you a list of resources.

What You Will Need

To use this book most successfully, you will need:

- An IBM or IBM-compatible PC so you can perform the operations as they are described;

- A copy of the DOS operating system (either PC-DOS or MS-DOS), which you might have to purchase separately from your computer dealer; and

- A little time. We have given you only the essentials—you will still need some time to try it all out.

This book uses an IBM PC/AT for examples that depend on a particular type of PC. If you have a different kind of IBM PC or a compatible PC from a computer manufacturer other than IBM, you may see slightly different messages or a key or control may be in a slightly different place. However, you should have no problem following the exercises.

We also assume you are using version 5.0 of DOS. If you are using another version, you should still be able to perform the exercises. The messages displayed on the screen may be different or a file we ask you to use may not be available. Use the examples we give you as models rather than performing them exactly.

If you want to sit down and use your PC for the first time, you are probably faced with one of two situations: the PC is cabled, connected, plugged in, and ready to go; or you are looking at a couple of large cardboard boxes and wondering where to start. If you need help putting your computer together, go to Appendix A where we tell you everything you need to know about setting up your PC.

Once that is done, you are ready for Chapter 1, which introduces you to the parts of your PC and talks about the different ways you can use it.

Part I

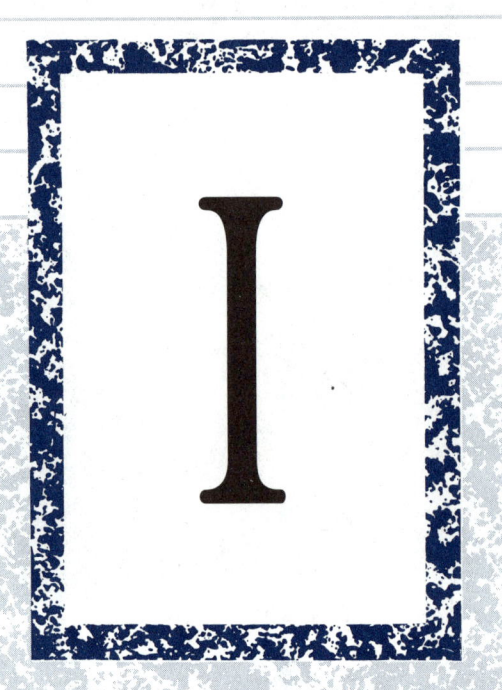

An Introduction to Your PC

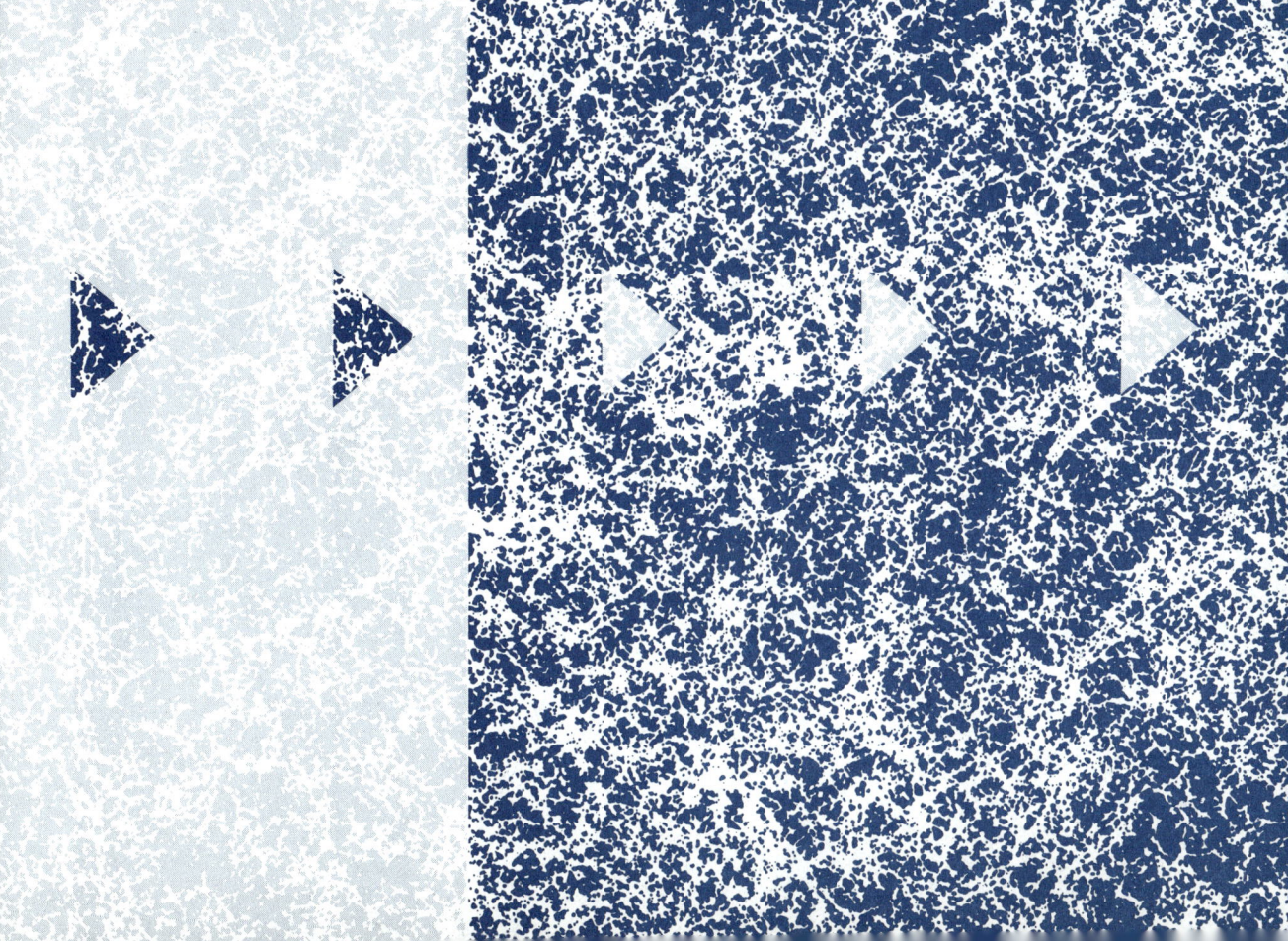

Chapter 1

> Anatomy of Your PC

*F*eaturing

Basic hardware components

386 type computers

Software overview

You probably already know that computers consist of both hardware and software. The *hardware* is the machine itself; the *software* is the information you use with it. A useful analogy is your stereo system; the stereo components are the equivalent of your computer's hardware, and the music (recorded on compact discs, tapes, and record albums) is the equivalent of software.

Let's begin by identifying the hardware components of your PC, as shown in Figure 1.1. Not all PCs have identical components, but most have the same basic components. In this chapter, we discuss those basic components. Refer to Chapter 10 for additional components that your PC may have.

*H*ardware

*T*he System Unit

The *system unit* is really the computer itself. It performs all operations, calculations, and processes; that is why it is often called the *central processing unit* or CPU. Inside are the electronic components, the microprocessor and printed-circuit boards that make the PC work.

The system unit contains the PC's *memory*. Memory is where your PC stores information and instructions as it processes them. Some information and instructions are stored permanently, and some are loaded into memory from a disk to be stored in memory temporarily. Temporary storage can be programs, such as the operating system or application software, or it can be the reports or information you use with the programs. Since your PC's memory capacity is limited, these programs and data are stored on your PC's hard or floppy disks when they are not being used, so that they do not take up valuable memory space.

The Hard Disk Drive

The system unit also contains your PC's *hard disk drive*, also known as a *fixed disk drive*. The hard disk drive consists of a hard

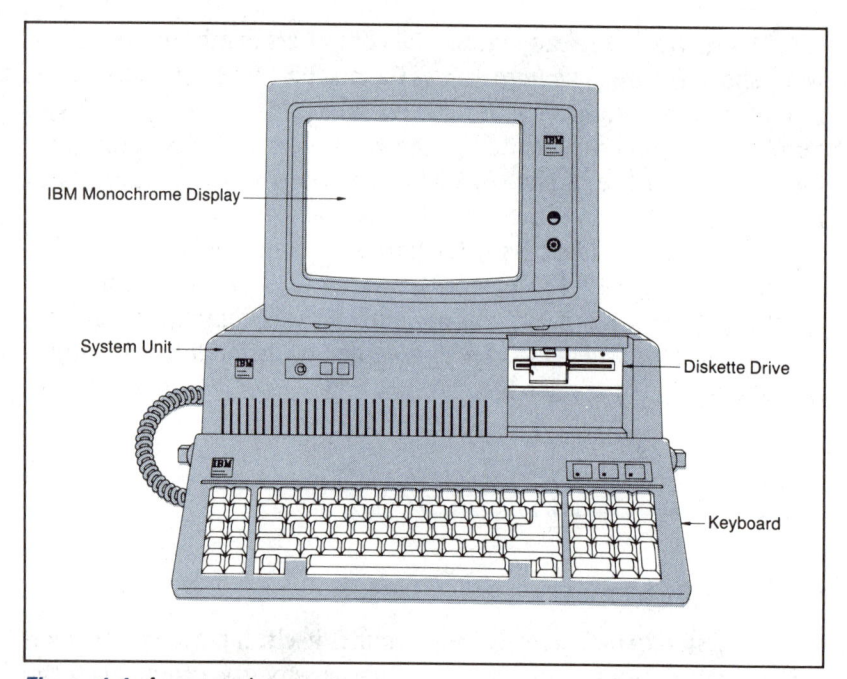

Figure 1.1: *A personal computer*

disk, a mechanism that spins the disk, a head that reads information from and writes information to the hard disk, and the electronics that make the disk drive work. The hard disk is sealed within the drive. As the hard disk spins within the drive, the head reads information from it and records information onto it.

Your hard disk stores the software you use with your PC. The hard disk contains the operating system programs that tell your PC how to work. As you work with your PC, you will also store application programs and information files on the hard disk.

The Keyboard

You communicate with your PC by typing instructions and pressing keys on the *keyboard*. There are actually several types of PC keyboards. IBM produced three types: the original IBM PC and IBM PC/XT keyboard (see Figure 1.2), the IBM PC/AT keyboard (see Figure 1.3), and the enhanced keyboard for the PC/XT and PC/AT (see Figure 1.4). Although the layout of the keys are different on the three keyboards, each has all of the keys you will need to use. Find the one that best matches yours.

You will notice that the main part of the keyboard is much like a typewriter. The extra keys are used to perform special operations, sometimes alone and sometimes in conjunction with other keys.

If you can't find a key when we show it in a later illustration, refer back to the illustration of your keyboard on this page. From now on, we will assume you are using the enhanced keyboard.

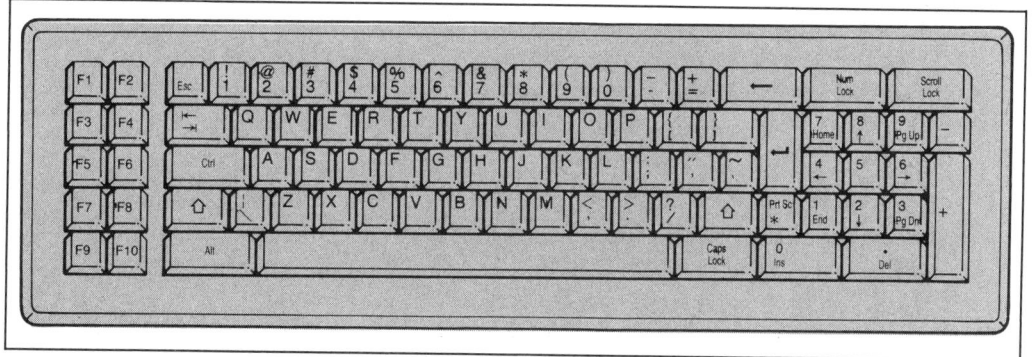

Figure 1.2: *The original IBM PC keyboard*

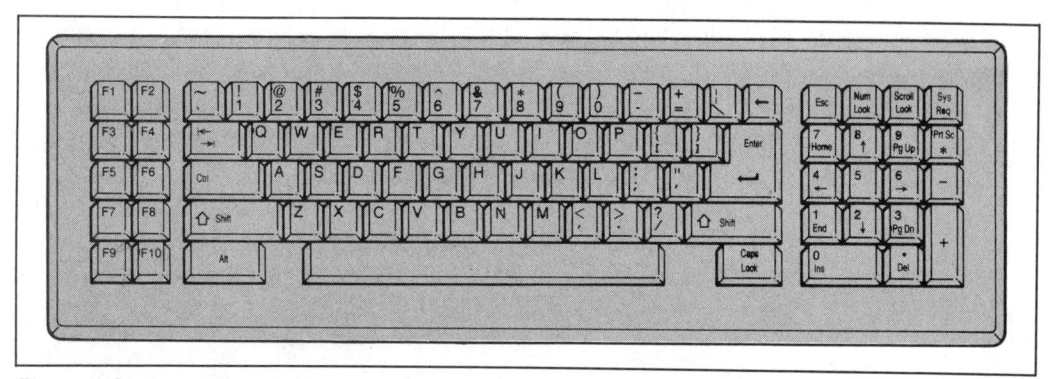

Figure 1.3: The IBM PC/AT keyboard

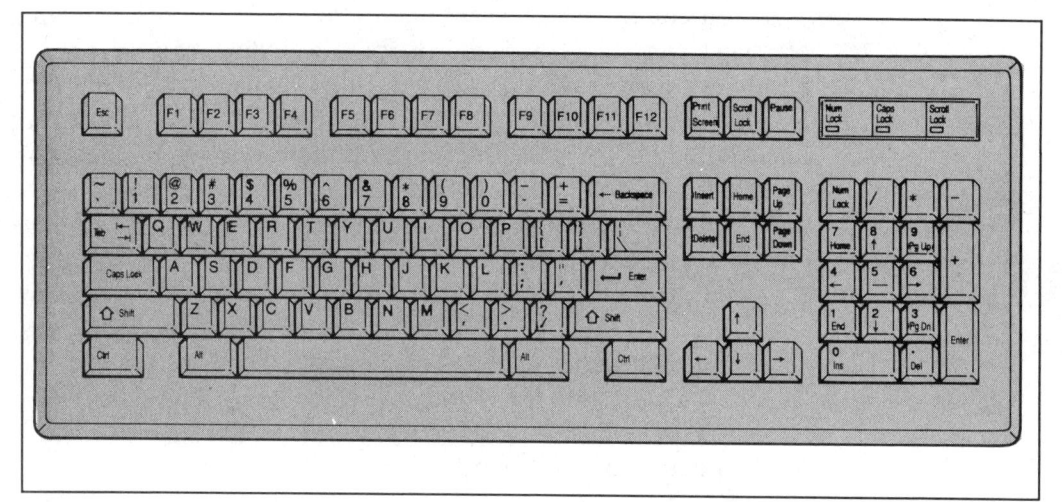

Figure 1.4: The enhanced keyboard

If you are familiar with a typewriter or other keyboard, you know that one key sometimes serves two purposes. For example, you type 5 if you want a 5 but you hold down the Shift key and type 5 if you want a % sign. Many keys on the PC keyboard are used like the Shift key, giving different results when used with another key. You will learn about these keys throughout this book, especially in Chapter 3.

The keyboard itself is designed to be tilted or level, and is easily adjusted with the knobs on either side.

The Diskette Drive

A *diskette drive* or *floppy disk drive* transfers information to and from your hard disk or directly into memory. Diskette drives read and record information on diskettes. Unlike your hard disk drive and hard disk, which are one unit, diskette drives and diskettes are separate; you can insert and remove diskettes from a diskette drive. You don't use diskettes to store information that you use often because diskette drives are slower and hold much less information than your hard disk. Instead, you can use diskettes to transfer information to and from your PC's hard disk. For example, software manufacturers distribute programs on diskette. You use such distribution diskettes to copy programs to your hard disk. Diskettes are also a good way to transfer information from your PC to another or to store copies of the information on your hard disk.

This book assumes that you have a hard disk and one diskette drive. The diskette drive is called A:, and the hard disk is called C:. They are not labeled, so you will just have to remember which is which. However, you will use them so often that remembering won't be much of a problem.

If your PC does not have a hard disk drive, you can store all of your information on diskettes. Appendix B gives you additional instructions for using a PC with no hard disk.

The Display

Different people call the display by different names. You might hear it referred to as a monitor, console, CRT (cathode ray tube), VDT (video display terminal), terminal, or, simply, screen. Whatever you call it, its function is to display what you type on the keyboard, give you instructions, ask you questions, and present you with information.

Your computer does not need a display to do its job, but *you* need it so that you have an idea of what is going on. Without a display, you do not know what you are typing and your PC has no way to communicate with you. A display is really more of a necessity than an option, although it is often purchased separately. In addition to the display, you need an adapter that plugs into your PC.

For simplicity, we assume that you have an EGA or VGA display, but you can use other displays, including a regular home TV set. If you want to use the PC with your TV set, you will have to buy a special adapter, called an RF modulator, to convert the signal that the PC puts out into one that the TV can understand. Consult your PC operations guide for more information.

The knobs on the front of the display are used to adjust the contrast and brightness of the screen, just like a TV. On your display, the controls may not be on the front.

The Mouse

Your PC may also have a *mouse*, like the one shown in Figure 1.5. Your PC's mouse is not an animal, but a small device that sits to the side of your keyboard. Some programs use the mouse to control a pointer on the display. You move the pointer by moving the mouse on your desk. If you move the mouse to the right, the pointer moves to the right; if you move the mouse to the left, the pointer moves to the left; and so on. You might use the pointer to draw and move shapes in a graphics program, or to select text and commands in a word processing program.

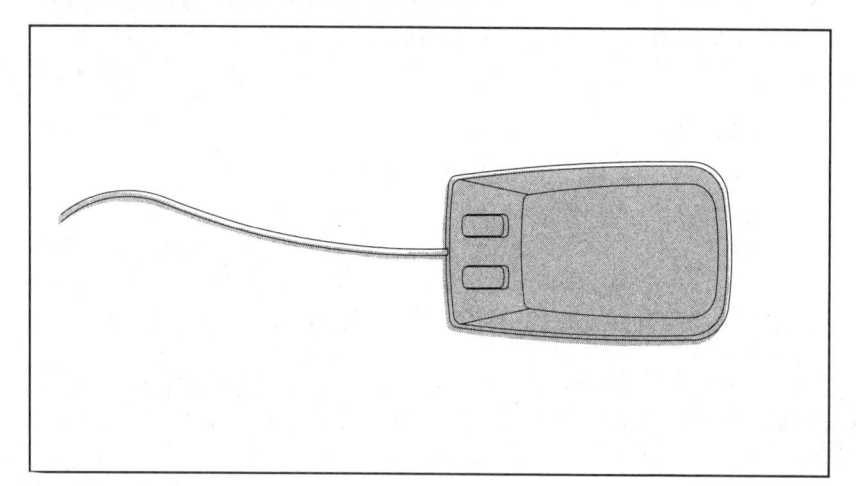

Figure 1.5: A Mouse

How 386 Computers Are Different

This book is written for all users of IBM PC type computers, including PC/XT, PC/AT1, and 386 class machines. The most important difference between these types of computers is in their *central processing units,* or *CPU*s. The CPU is the main chip in your computer—it's responsible for interpreting and executing instructions and generally managing the operations of the computer:

- original IBM PC and PC/XT type computers have 8086 or 8088 CPUs
- PC/AT class computers have 80286 CPUs
- 386 type computers have 80386 or 80486 CPUs

There are many differences between these CPUs. Perhaps the most important to you are their different capabilities in the areas of speed, power, and memory management.

In the sense that we are using them here, *speed* refers to how fast a CPU can move bits around, and *power* refers to how many bits it can move at a time. What it all boils down to is that the later CPUs (386s and 486s) are generally faster and more powerful than earlier ones. This means that a 386 computer, for example, will usually run programs faster than a computer with an earlier CPU. You should be aware, however, that there can be major differences among CPUs of the same general type. For example, different versions of 386 CPUs run at 12 MHz, 16MHz, 20MHz, and 33MHz. Depending on the programs that you use, these variances in speed could be quite important to you.

CPUs of the 386 class have significantly better *memory management* capabilities than do their predecessors. This means that they can control more memory and do more things with it. Powerful software often demands sophisticated memory management. One example is Windows 3.0, which runs much better on 386 class computers.

Expansion Slots

Inside your computer's system unit are *expansion slots*. These are connectors to which you can attach *expansion boards* or *cards* in order to add features to your system. Expansion slots, and the boards that you plug into them, are divided into the same classes as CPUs—there are 8-bit, 16-bit, and 32-bit slots. In today's computers, 16-bit slots are the most common. Most of the slots in a 386 computer will usually be 16-bit, even though the CPU is a 32-bit microprocessor. Slots for 16-bit and 32-bit boards look the same, so you should consult the documentation for your computer if you are adding a board and aren't sure where to put it. You won't have any problem distinguishing 8-bit slots—they're quite a bit shorter than the others. In addition, you can use an 8-bit expansion board even if you don't have an 8-bit slot. Just plug the board into a 16-bit slot—it will work fine.

Software

You will be using two kinds of software with your PC: the disk operating system, and application programs. A third kind, called an operating environment, is optional. You store software on your hard disk and on diskettes.

The Disk Operating System

The *disk operating system* coordinates the interaction between the hardware and software, most importantly the transfer of information between the memory in the system unit and the disk drives (which are sometimes called external memory). It also coordinates other activities such as printing.

Your PC uses an operating system called DOS (or more formally PC-DOS or MS-DOS, depending on who sold it to you). Even though you cannot operate your computer without DOS, you may not receive a copy of it when you purchase your PC. If that is the case, you have to buy it separately.

Operating Environments

Operating environments are programs that change the way you interact with your PC. Two of the most popular are Microsoft Windows and the *Shell* that comes with DOS 5. Normally, you interact with your PC by typing DOS commands, loading an application program, and working with one file at a time. Operating environment programs let you work with several applications and files at the same time. Usually, they display files in *windows* on your screen. Windows, shown in Figure 1.6, are like sheets of paper; you can move them, change their size, and stack them on top of each other. Instead of typing commands, you use a mouse to select commands from menus and manipulate the windows on your screen.

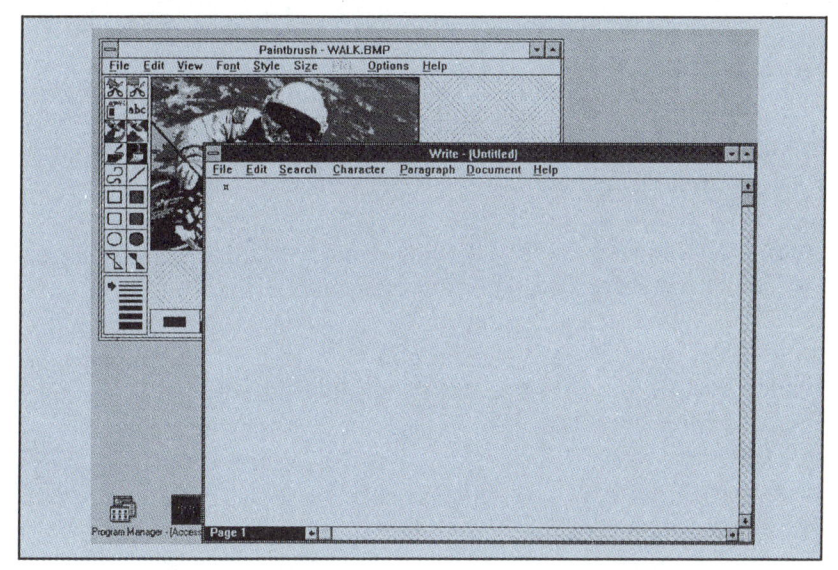

Figure 1.6: A Windows screen

If you have a program such as Microsoft Windows on your PC or you using the DOS 5 shell, you can use the DOS prompt to follow the examples in this book and learn about DOS. Read the documentation that came with the program to learn how to display the DOS prompt.

Application Programs

Application programs operate in conjunction with DOS so that you can perform useful tasks with your PC without having to be a programmer. There are thousands of application programs available that convert your PC into a tool to increase productivity and decrease paperwork. The most popular programs can be grouped into six categories: word processors, spreadsheets, database management programs, payroll and accounting programs, graphics, and desktop publishing. A seventh category, games, converts your PC into an entertainment center.

Chances are, if you are using your PC at home or in the office, you will be using one or more of these kinds of programs. So let's take a look at what each of them can do for you.

Word Processors

Word processors turn your PC into a super typewriter. Currently, the most popular word processing program is WordPerfect—we introduce you to it in Chapter 9.

With a word processor you compose text using your PC keyboard just as you would use a typewriter keyboard. However, because the characters are recorded electronically rather than on paper, you can correct your mistakes and make any changes you want before printing the text out on a printer. You can erase words, phrases, or whole blocks of text, insert new ones, or move them from one place to another with a few keystrokes. Then you can store your document on a diskette and go back to it at any time. You can print it or revise it whenever you want, or you can copy it and store multiple versions of the same document.

One of the real benefits of word-processing programs is that you can view your document on your PC's display before printing it out. If you don't like what you see, you can change margins, line spacing, or tab settings and see the effect immediately on the screen. This is called *on-screen formatting*. You see only the portion of the document that can fit on your screen at one time, but that does not mean that the size of your document is limited to the size of your screen. You can move backwards and forwards through the document as you wish, looking at a page or section at a time. This is called *paging* or *scrolling*.

In some offices, a few PCs may be used only for word processing. These dedicated machines are probably in the hands of secretaries who can really make them produce. However, because of word processing, typing is no longer just for secretaries. Many office professionals use word processors to compose reports or letters and to jot off memos or notes. In addition, a large group of professional writers feel that their wildest dreams have come true!

Spreadsheets

We talk about spreadsheets in more detail in Chapter 9, so we will just give you a brief introduction here.

All electronic spreadsheets are based on the same idea. You are given an electronic worksheet or grid made up of rows and columns. The intersection of each row and column is called a cell. You can set up a typical financial report or model by entering column and row labels such as Sales, Expenses, or Profit and the appropriate data—either numbers or formulas. The numbers represent variables and the formulas maintain their relationship between the variables. If the values (numbers) change, all related values change. If you change a variable value, all related values change on the basis of the formula. If you change the relationship by changing the formula, again, all affected entries are changed.

Spreadsheets make it easy to play the *What If?* game. Once your model is established, you can use it to see the potential effect of different decisions. What if expenses increase? What if sales decrease? What about expanding? Where is the breakeven point? At home, you can analyze stock purchase decisions, figure your income tax, or decide whether it is more cost effective to rent or buy that piece of equipment.

Lotus 1-2-3 is currently the most popular PC spreadsheet. However, its popularity has spawned lots of similar products, many of which you can use with your PC.

Database Management Programs

Databases are large pools of information, which can be numbers or text. You can use a database management program to search for a particular piece of information, to find all information in the database fitting certain criteria, or to sort the information in specified ways. Databases can be used with other programs such as word processors or spreadsheets.

Databases can be extremely large, such as one an airline uses for issuing passengers' tickets, or very small, such as one that keeps a list of the employees in your department.

Two popular database programs are dBASE and R:BASE. Both programs allow you to collect and categorize information, and then retrieve it in different forms. However, they each do some things better than others, so you need to pick the product best suited to your project.

Payroll and Accounting Programs

If you run a small business, you can use an accounting application for your payroll, accounts payable and receivable, and general ledger. If you have the kind of business where everyone wears lots of hats, computerized accounting can free up time to focus on the business of the business rather than the bookkeeping.

In the past, many small businesses have bought accounting services from a bank or computer service center. With a PC, you can buy an application program (for example, DacEasy) and do your own accounting, probably for less money.

Graphics

Graphics programs let you display information as a graph or chart. You can display pie charts, bar and line graphs, or scattergrams. Graphics programs make it easy to summarize large amounts of data or to identify trends. Often graphs are used in reports or as presentation aids.

Graphics programs are very useful; however, they require special hardware. For example, you must add a special graphics board to your system unit as well as a graphics monitor (usually a color monitor). In addition, you may need to buy a special printer or plotter so that you can make a copy on paper of the graph or chart that is displayed on your screen.

Desktop Publishing

Desktop publishing programs let you produce documents that look like they came off a printing press. You can combine different styles and sizes of text with graphics on the same page. Such programs use a graphics display to show your document. What you see on your screen is exactly what you get when you print your document with a high-quality printer. You don't have to be a magazine or newspaper publisher to benefit from using a desktop publishing program. With desktop publishing, you can produce impressive-looking reports, proposals, and newsletters.

Two popular desktop publishing programs are Ventura Publisher and PageMaker. Each operates differently. If you plan to do desktop publishing, you should take a look at the type of documents you will produce and determine what capabilities you require before you choose a program.

Games

At home, games are a popular use for the PC. Like everything else, some are good and some are bad—the choice is pretty broad. Some of the best games include animation and lively graphics as well as different levels of expertise.

While games do not generally help get the job done at the office, they are good forms of relaxation and some people feel they sharpen problem-solving skills and hand-eye coordination.

Now that you know what you will be working with in terms of both hardware and software, you are ready to begin using your PC.

Review

Your computer has the following hardware components:

- The system unit
- The hard disk
- The keyboard
- The diskette drives
- The display

There are three kinds of PC software:

- Disk operating systems
- Operating environments
- Application programs

There are seven common types of application programs:

- Word processors
- Spreadsheets
- Database management programs
- Payroll and accounting programs
- Graphics
- Desktop publishing programs
- Games

Chapter 2

Beginning with the Basics

*F*eaturing

Setting the date and time

Typing and making corrections

The diskette drive

The keyboard

Now that you are familiar with the parts of your PC and have an idea of some of the things you can do with it, you are ready to start using your PC for the first time. But before you go any further, check two things:

- Is your PC plugged in?
- Has DOS been installed on your hard disk? Most computer dealers will install it for you when you purchase your PC.

Yes to both questions? If DOS has not been installed, find someone to do it for you. Although your DOS reference manual gives you instructions for preparing your hard disk and installing DOS on it, this can be a complicated process. It is better to have an expert do it for you.

*T*urning On Your PC

Turning on your PC is just a matter of following these steps:

① Turn the knobs on the front of the display fully to the right (your monitor may not have these controls in the front).

These are the contrast and brightness knobs. Once your PC is warmed up, you can adjust them, but if you don't start with them fully on, you might not see anything on the screen.

② Turn on the power with the switch on the right side or front of the system unit (some PCs have the power switch on the back).

Your PC runs through a quick test to make sure everything is in working order. If the test is successful, you hear a short beep. Next you see information about the version of DOS that your computer is loading.

Setting the Date and Time

When you load DOS, your PC may ask you for the current date and time by displaying the following message:

Current date is Mon 06-10-1991
Enter new date (mm-dd-yy):_

If your PC enters the date and time automatically, you won't see this message. Instead your PC will load DOS and immediately display the DOS prompt or the DOS shell. The DOS prompt is described later in this chapter, and the DOS shell is described in Chapter 6. Read the instructions for setting the date and time anyway. They show you how to enter information into your PC.

You do not have to set the date and time, but doing so now can prove useful later on. Then, when you store information in a file, DOS automatically stores the precise date and time with the file. Should you have more than one version of the same file, you can check the date later to see which version is most current. If you have not set the date, the existing date will be used as the date for every file.

The most common way to enter the date is month/day/year, as in 4/12/91, though 4-12-91 is also acceptable. You can use several formats for the date and time, but some are not acceptable. For example, July 4th will not work since DOS accepts only numbers in the date. Time is usually entered as hours:minutes or hours:minutes:seconds, as in 10:05 or

Beginning with the Basics   21

15:45:24. You can also add hundredths of seconds. Refer to your DOS reference manual for a list of all the acceptable formats.

If you use a format that is not acceptable, DOS flashes Invalid date or Invalid time on the screen and lets you try again.

Your PC is waiting for you to enter a new date so go ahead and type in today's date immediately after Enter new date:. For example,

Enter new date (mm-dd-yy): 6-25-91

The Cursor

The blinking underscore you see after date: is called the *cursor*. It marks the position on the screen where the next character you type will appear. You will see the cursor move about as you enter and change information. In a moment, we will tell you how to make the cursor move wherever you want it to (see the section "The Numeric Keypad and the Arrow Keys").

Correcting Mistakes

If you make a mistake, press the Backspace key (←) to go back to the point of the error and retype correctly (see Figure 2.1). Notice

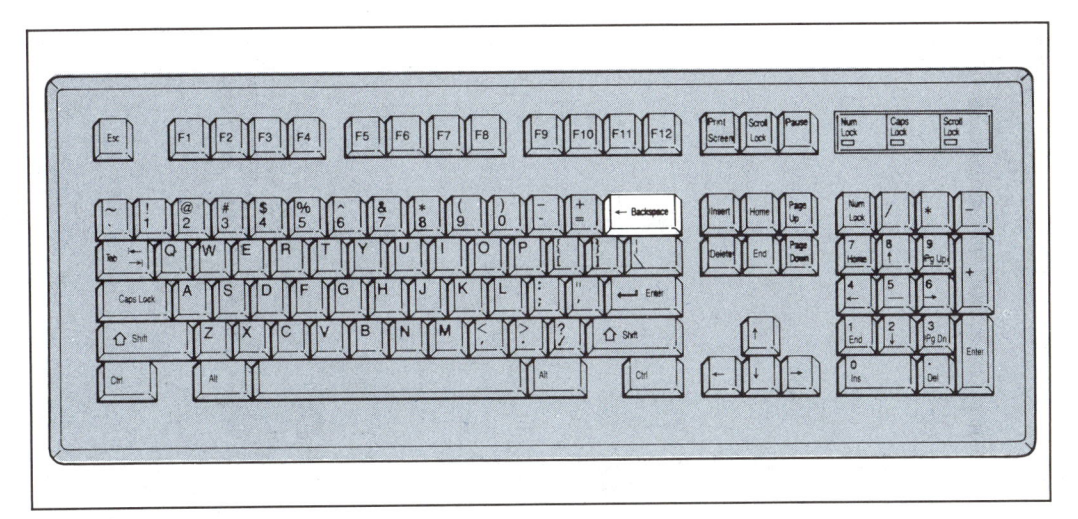

Figure 2.1: The Backspace key

that each time you press ←, the character to the left of the cursor is erased and the cursor moves back one space. In this way, you can backspace over an error to erase it, then retype the correct characters. If you are a perfect typist, you might want to make some deliberate mistakes so that you can practice erasing them.

*E*ntering *What You Have Typed*

The Enter key (←┘) on your PC keyboard replaces the Return key on a typewriter keyboard (see Figure 2.2). Sometimes you will use it like the Return key, but usually you will use it to enter an instruction into the computer. Although the information you type on the keyboard is displayed on the screen, the computer has no knowledge of it until you enter it by pressing ←┘ to finalize the operation.

① When you are satisfied that your typing is flawless, enter the date by pressing ←┘.

② If you do not want to set the date, just press ←┘ without typing anything.

③ Your PC displays the current-time message. For example,

**Current time is 7:44:02.33a
Enter new time:_**

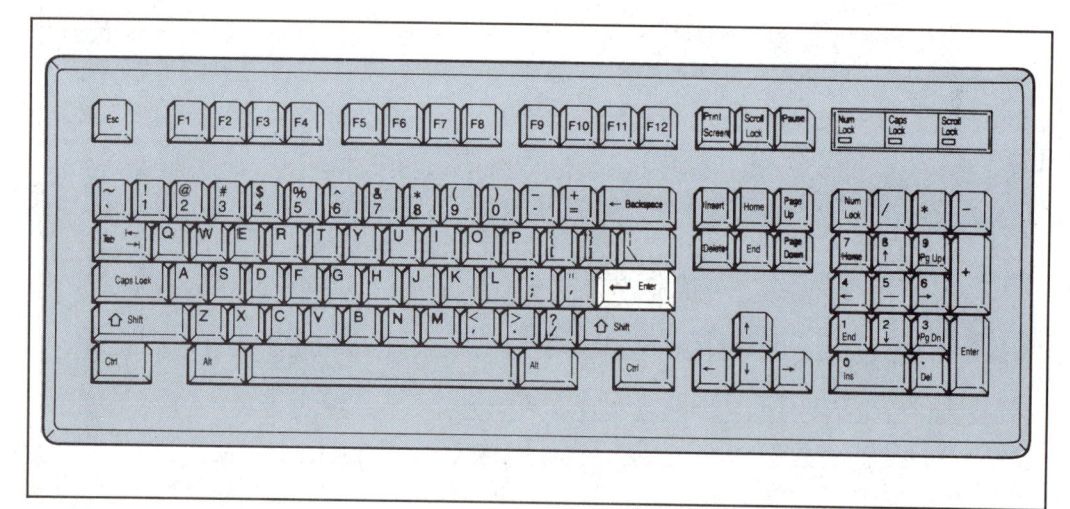

Figure 2.2: *The Enter key (←┘)*

④ Type the time after Enter new time:. For example,

   Enter new time: 15:30:00

⑤ If you typed the time correctly, press ⏎ to enter it.

⑥ If you do not want to set the time, just press ⏎ without typing anything.

⑦ At this point the DOS prompt appears on the screen. It looks like this:

   C>

The DOS Prompt

Once DOS is loaded and the date and time are set, your screen displays C> or the DOS shell. This is the *DOS prompt*, sometimes called the C prompt, and it tells you that DOS has been loaded successfully.

The C tells you that DOS is using drive C: as the current drive—unless you tell it otherwise, it will always expect to find the information it needs on your hard disk—drive C:. The > symbol says *OK, I'm ready. Tell me what to do next.* That is why it is called a *prompt;* it is prompting you for the next instruction.

Using the Diskette Drive

Your PC is useless to you without software to make it do what you want. You load software onto your PC's hard disk by copying it from a diskette. Therefore, it is important to know how to insert and remove diskettes. Let's practice.

Inserting a Diskette

① Find your DOS operating diskette. This is one of the diskettes your dealer used to install DOS on your hard disk. In case you accidentally lose the information on your hard disk, you can use this diskette to reinstall DOS. You should find this diskette in a plastic holder in the back of your DOS reference manual.

② Hold the diskette with the label up, right thumb on the label, and slide it out of its paper sleeve. Be careful not to touch the surfaces that are exposed through the cutouts on the diskette jacket. (If you are lost already, take a look at Figure 2.3.)

③ Open the door of your diskette drive if it is not already open.

④ Push the diskette gently into the drive, being careful not to bend it. Make sure it is fully inserted.

⑤ Close the drive door.

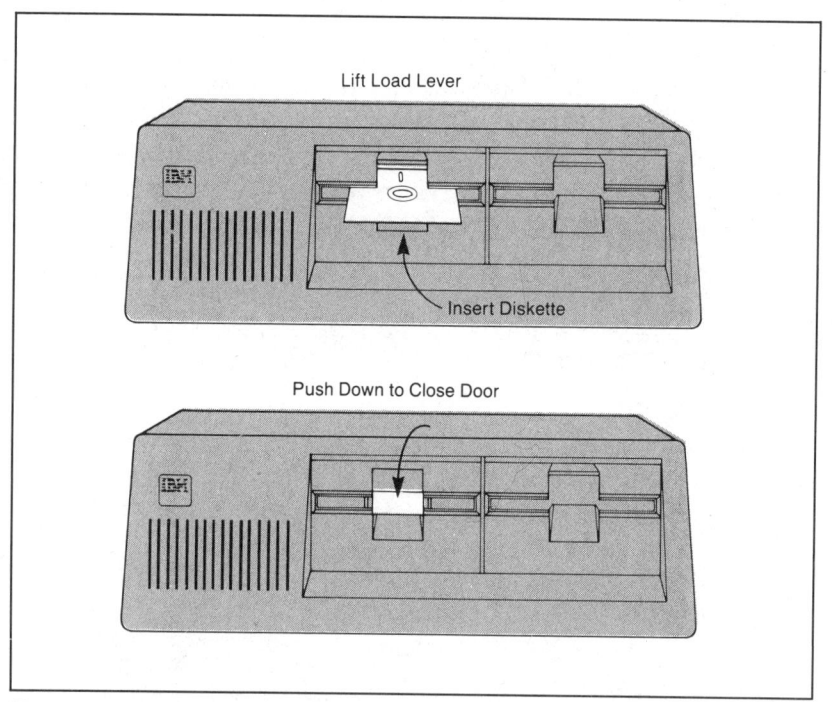

Figure 2.3: Inserting a diskette

Changing the Current Drive in the DOS Shell

Remember that DOS is installed on your hard disk, drive C:. When you turn on your PC, drive C: is the current drive. You might decide to put a diskette in your diskette drive, drive A:, and start working with it instead. In that case, there would be no point in keeping drive C: as the current drive.

If you are using the DOS 5 shell, changing to drive A: couldn't be easier—just click the icon for this drive. After you click it, the icon will be highlighted. When you want to return to drive C:, click its icon.

Changing the Current Drive with the DOS Prompt

To move to drive A: using the DOS prompt, you are going to have to type A:. Use the shift key to type a colon (:) just as you would on a typewriter.

The Shift Keys

The ⇧ shift keys on your PC keyboard replace the Shift keys on a typewriter keyboard (see Figure 2.4). As with a typewriter, you can use them to type capital letters, symbols such as %, and some punctuation marks, including :.

Now practice moving from one drive to another.

① The last line on your screen reads

C>

You move to drive A: by typing A: ⏎ immediately after C>. The last line now reads

C>A:

This changes the DOS prompt to A> and tells DOS to look at the diskette in drive A: for further instructions. This is sometimes called logging onto drive A: and drive A: then becomes the *logged* or *default* drive.

② When you are ready to go back to drive C:, immediately after A> type C: ↵. The last line now reads

A>C:

The DOS prompt C> reappears, indicating that drive C: is the current (or logged) drive once again.

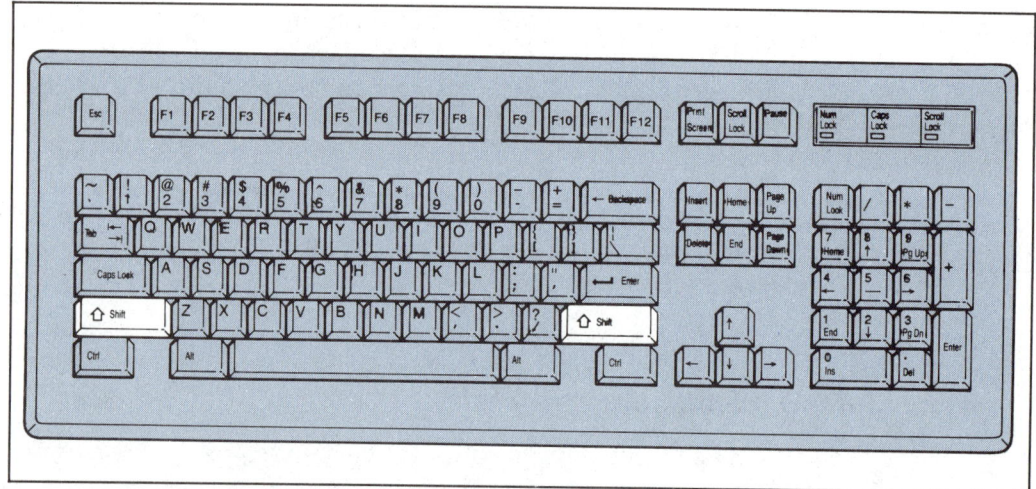

Figure 2.4: The Shift keys

Removing a Diskette

Now, remove the diskette.

① Open the drive door.

② Remove the diskette without bending it or touching the exposed surfaces.

③ Replace the diskette in its paper sleeve.

Keep the DOS diskette nearby. You will use it in the next chapter when we show you commands for your PC.

Getting Familiar with the Keyboard

As you have realized by now, you communicate with your IBM PC by typing on the keyboard. You can enter commands and information, respond to prompts, and select different options or functions. All your word-processing and spreadsheet reports will be entered from the keyboard, as well as any information you want to use with other application programs.

Your PC keyboard is arranged similarly to a typewriter keyboard. Most of the keys are marked just as they are on a typewriter with a few notable exceptions. You already know about the Enter key (⏎), the Backspace key (←), and the Shift key (⇧). The Tab key, which works like a typewriter Tab key, is marked ⇆. But what are all those other keys?

There are three additional sets of keys on the PC keyboard that you will not find on a typewriter keyboard: the numeric keypad, including the cursor-positioning (arrow) keys; the function keys; and several control keys, the most important of which, for right now, are the Ctrl and Esc keys.

The Numeric Keypad and the Arrow Keys

When you press the key marked Num Lock (see Figure 2.5), you can use the numeric keypad located on the right of your keyboard to enter numbers. If you are going to use application programs that require lots of numbers, the numeric pad can be very handy, especially if you already know how to operate a ten-key calculator by touch.

When the Num Lock key is off (simply press it again to turn it off), you can use the keys marked with an arrow to position the cursor. The arrow keys move the cursor up, down, to the right, and to the left. You can also use the keys marked Home, PgUp, PgDown, and End to move the cursor. These keys can have a special meaning for different application programs you may be using. Be sure to consult the reference manual for that program to find out what they mean.

When Num Lock is on, you can't use the arrow or other cursor movement keys. For that reason, IBM has provided a duplicate set of

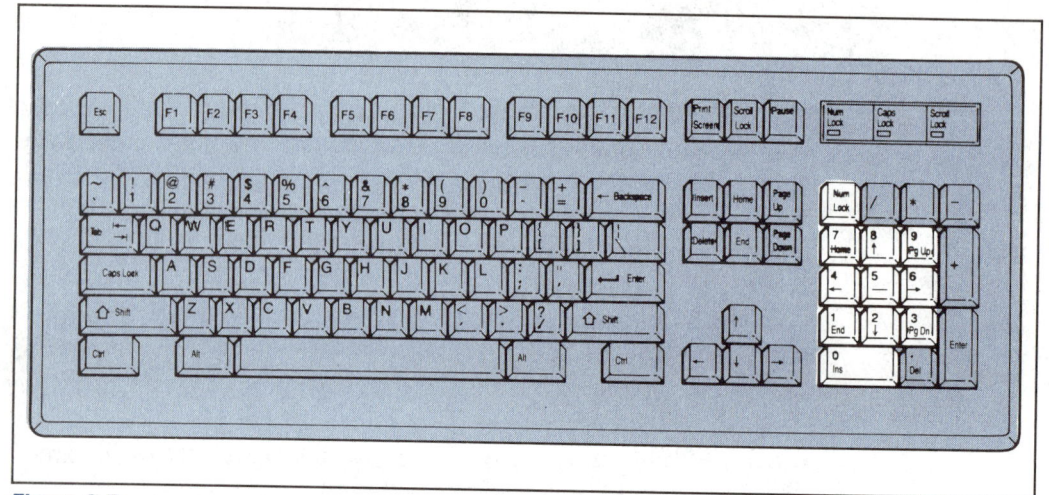

Figure 2.5: The Numeric keypad, the arrow keys, and the Num Lock key

cursor keys on the enhanced keyboard (located between the standard keyboard and the numeric keypad). You may find it more convenient to use these cursor movement keys all of the time, even when Num Lock is off.

The Function Keys

Figure 2.6 shows the twelve function keys (F1 to F12) positioned at the top of your keyboard. If you have an older keyboard, your ten function keys will be grouped together on the left. These keys perform predefined tasks that change from application to application. We will tell you more about them when we show you how to tell your PC what to do.

The Ctrl Key

Remember that we said in Chapter 1 that some keys are used with other keys to add another dimension to your keyboard? For example, the key marked j becomes J when used with the Shift key. The Ctrl key (see Figure 2.7) works the same way.

Beginning with the Basics 29

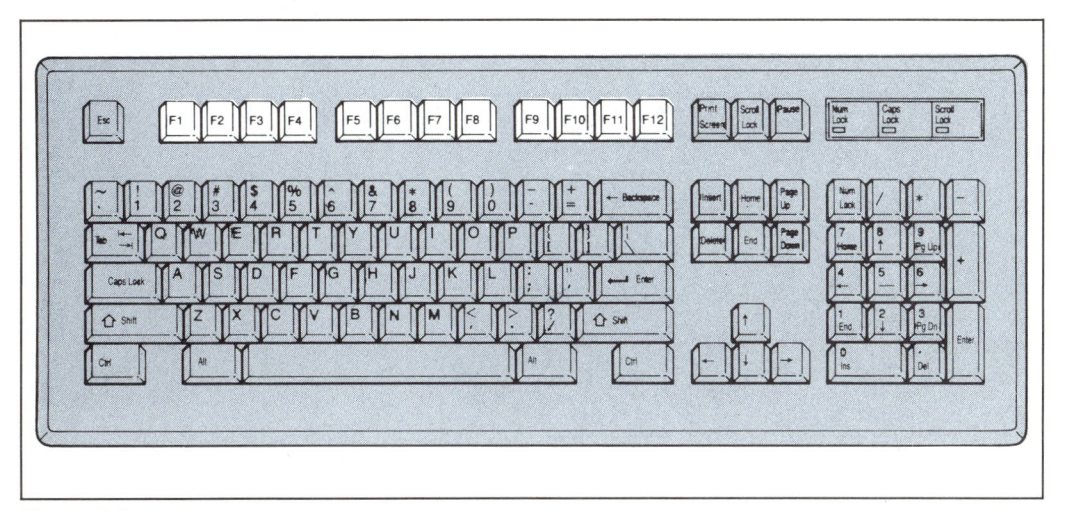

Figure 2.6: The function keys

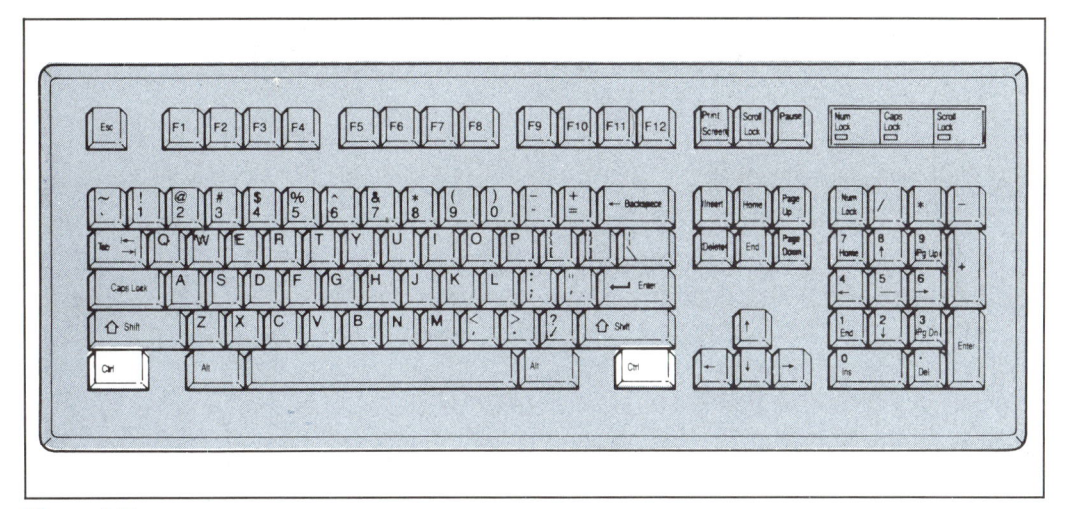

Figure 2.7: The Ctrl key

The Esc Key

The Esc (escape) key (see Figure 2.8) may perform different functions in different application programs, but basically it is used to get you out of situations you don't want to be in. It is also used to interrupt programs or commands. Some programs will ask you to confirm that you

Figure 2.8: The Esc key

really want to interrupt the process; others will assume that you know what you are doing. Check the program documentation to find out exactly how the Esc key works for that program.

Resetting Your PC

Your PC does not do anything without *your* instructions. However, you might accidentally type a wrong command or press a wrong key and lose control of what it is doing. There's no need to panic, you can always regain control by resetting your PC. Resetting your PC interrupts whatever it is doing and reloads DOS. If you reset from within an application, you may lose the information that you created since you last saved your file. If you save often, losing information is a small sacrifice compared to knowing that you are truly in control.

① As shown in Figure 2.9, hold down the Ctrl and Alt keys on the left of the keyboard, and press the Del key on the right. (Sound like a lot of keys to press at once? It is. You don't want to accidentally reset your PC.)

② Your PC loads DOS from the hard disk. When it finishes you may see the current-date message again. For example,

**Current date is Tue 07-09-1991
Enter new date (mm-dd-yy):_**

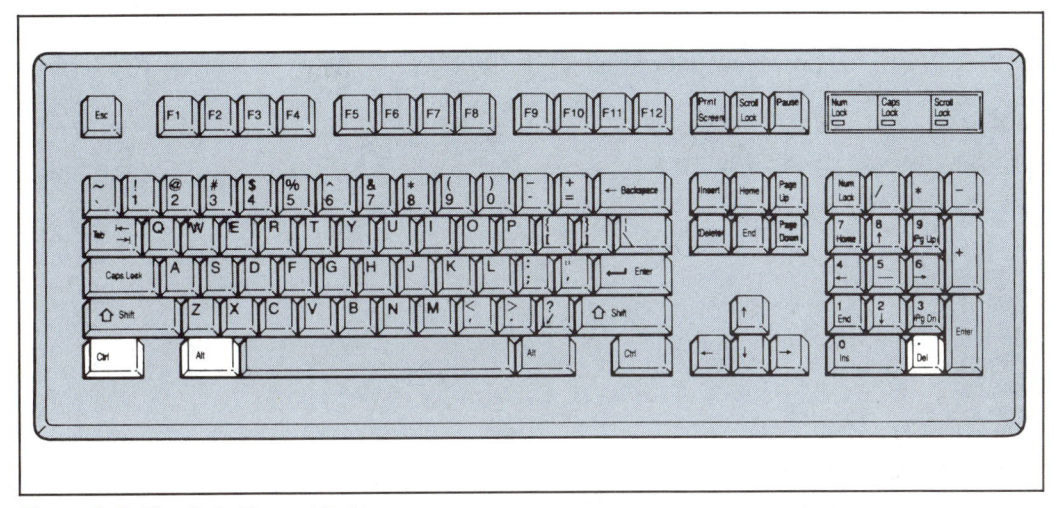

Figure 2.9: The Ctrl, Alt, and Del keys

Turning off Your PC

You turn off your PC by turning off the power switch. If you turn off your PC while the hard disk drive is in the process of reading or writing information on the hard disk, you could accidentally damage your hard disk. To prevent such damage, most PCs automatically shut down the hard disk before they turn off. Others give you a special command, called Shutdown or Park, for shutting down your hard disk before you turn off your PC. Check your operations manual for instructions on properly turning off your PC.

So that starts you out. You always turn on the machine, load DOS, and optionally set the date and time to begin. These steps will become second nature soon, but until they do, here is a quick review of the points in this chapter.

Review

To turn on the computer:

- Be sure the power cord is connected to the system unit and plugged into a live outlet.
- Turn on the power switch on the right side of the system unit.

To adjust the screen brightness:

- Use the knobs on the side of the keyboard to tilt or lower the keyboard.
- Use the knobs on the front of the display screen to adjust the brightness and contrast.

The date and time:

- Can be reset every time you turn on your PC.
- Can be saved with any files you store on disk.
- Allows you to check for the most current information.

To correct mistakes:

- Use the Backspace key (←).

To enter what you have typed:

- Use the Enter key (←⏎).

To insert a diskette in the diskette drive:

- Hold the diskette with the label up, right thumb on the label, and slide it out of its paper sleeve.
- Open the diskette drive door.
- Push the diskette gently into the drive.
- Close the drive door.

To change the current drive:

- Click the icon for the drive you want (in DOS 5) or type the drive identifier (A or C) followed by a : (for example, C:).

Additional keys:

- The numeric keypad, including the cursor-positioning (arrow) keys
- The duplicate cursor movement keys
- The function keys
- The Ctrl key
- The Esc key

To reset your PC:

- Hold down the Ctrl and Alt keys, and press the Del key.

To turn off your PC:

- Check whether or not you need to shut down your hard disk separately.
- Turn off the power switch.

Part II

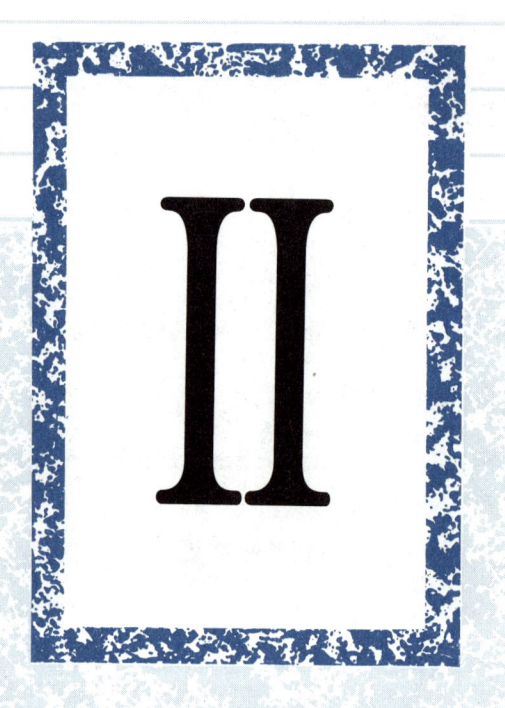

Using the DOS Command Line

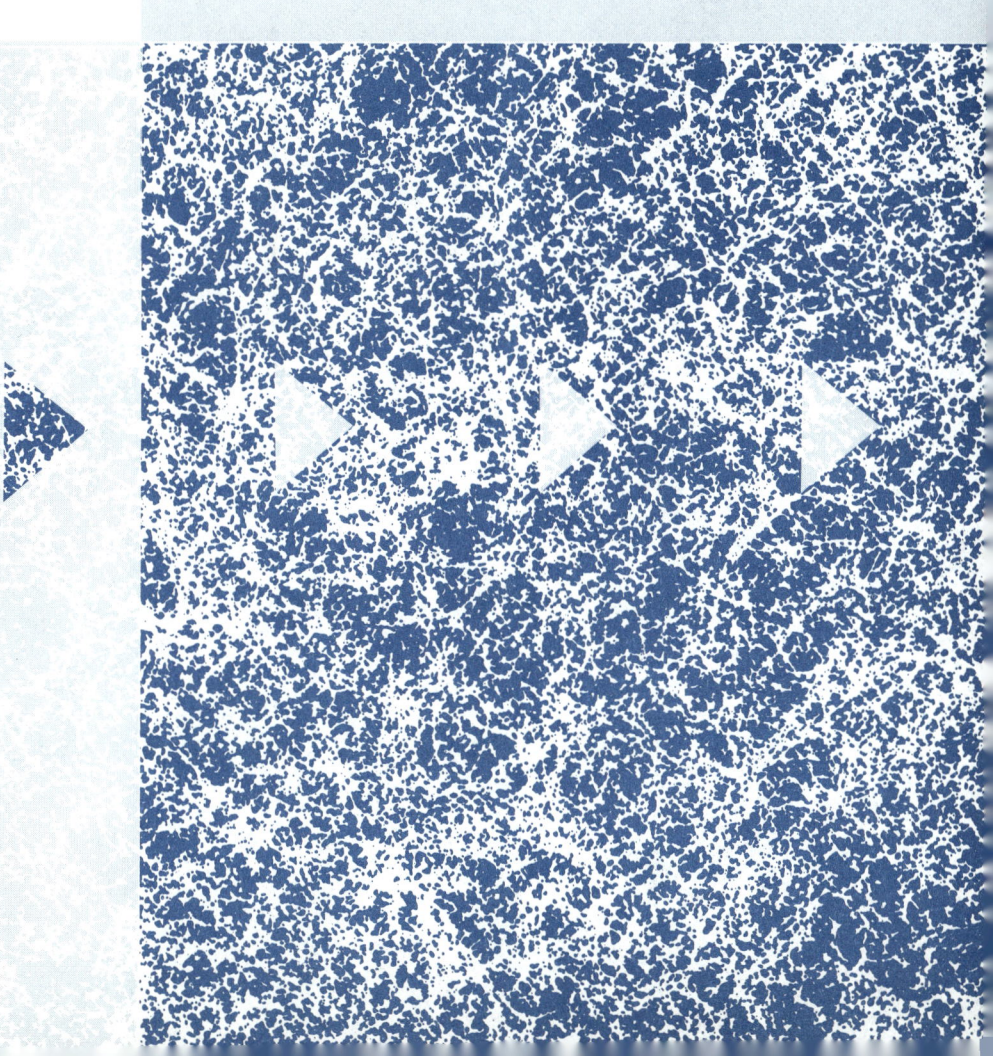

3

▶ Commands for Your PC

*F*eaturing

Canceling commands

Using menus

Using function keys

Your PC is a willing servant provided you tell it exactly what you want it to do. Today's reality doesn't let you speak to your PC; however, you can communicate easily and effectively by using commands.

Commands are typed, selected from a list of command options, or chosen by pressing the function key associated with the command. The method depends on the software that you are using. For example, DOS, your computer's operating system, responds to commands that you type.

*T*yping Commands

Typed commands are words that have special meanings. With them, you instruct your PC to perform specific tasks. Each software application has its own set of commands. However, once you become familiar with different applications, you will see that they have some commands in common.

The typed commands you use with your PC are related to the task you want the software to perform. Sometimes the command name directly reflects the task. For example, LIST, PRINT, and DELETE are common commands that are used with many software applications. However, most of the time the command is expressed in a kind of shorthand. The command DIR, for example, lists all the files in the directory and the command CHKDSK checks the amount of space available on the diskette. Occasionally the commands are not that easy to figure out—GRAFTABL, for example. (Don't worry about what that means for now.)

When you give instructions to people, you often have to give some extra information so that they know exactly what to do. For example, if you give the command *Go*, do you mean *Go to the store* or *Go to the movies?* Software commands are the same. You often have to give additional information so the computer will do exactly what you want.

The extra information you give when you enter a command is called a *parameter*. Each command has its own set of parameters for which you must supply specific values. For example, if you give your computer the command COPY, your computer needs to know *what* you want it to copy. The name of the file you want copied is a parameter of the command, and you would have to supply the file name in order for the command to be carried out.

Another thing about commands—you must enter them exactly as they are shown in the software's reference manual or the computer will not know what you mean. Type a command incorrectly and your PC will be stumped! It will flash a message like **Bad command name** or **File not found** at you and you will have to enter the command again.

That goes for parameters, too—you need to enter them in a precise way. Type them correctly, and enter them in the correct order. If you change the order, the computer will not know how to interpret the command, or will do something that you did not intend it to do.

We're going to try giving commands using the DOS command DIR as an example. The DIR command tells DOS to display a list of all the files stored on a disk or in a directory. DOS gives you the file name, the type of file, the size, and the date and time created. For example,

| APPEND | EXE | 5825 | 04-09-91 | 5:00a |
| ASSIGN | COM | 1561 | 04-09-91 | 5:00a |

ATTRIB	**EXE**	9529	04-09-91	5:00a
.	.	.	.	.
.	.	.	.	.
BASICA	**PIF**	2048	04-09-91	5:00a
MORTGAGE	**BAS**	6251	04-09-91	5:00a
32 File(s)	9216 bytes free			

It also tells you the total number of files on the disk; in this case, 32.

Want to give it a try? Because you may not have many files on your hard disk yet, let's list the files on the DOS operating diskette. Follow these steps:

① If it is not already on, turn on your PC now. Enter the date and time (if your PC does not do so automatically). When DOS has loaded, you see the C> prompt.

② Insert your DOS diskette into the diskette drive.

③ Change the current drive to the diskette drive. Immediately after the DOS prompt C>, type

　　A: ↵

④ Immediately after the A> prompt, type

　　DIR ↵

and watch what happens. Did the information move up off the screen faster than you could read it? When this happens, you will want to *freeze*, or stop, the display.

*F*reezing the Display

The display screen on your PC is really a window that shows only a portion of the information available to you. As you fill the screen with information it moves up, one line at a time, out of your view. This is called *scrolling*.

You can stop the display from scrolling out of view by using the Pause key (see Figure 3.1). Let's try it.

① Type:

　　DIR ↵

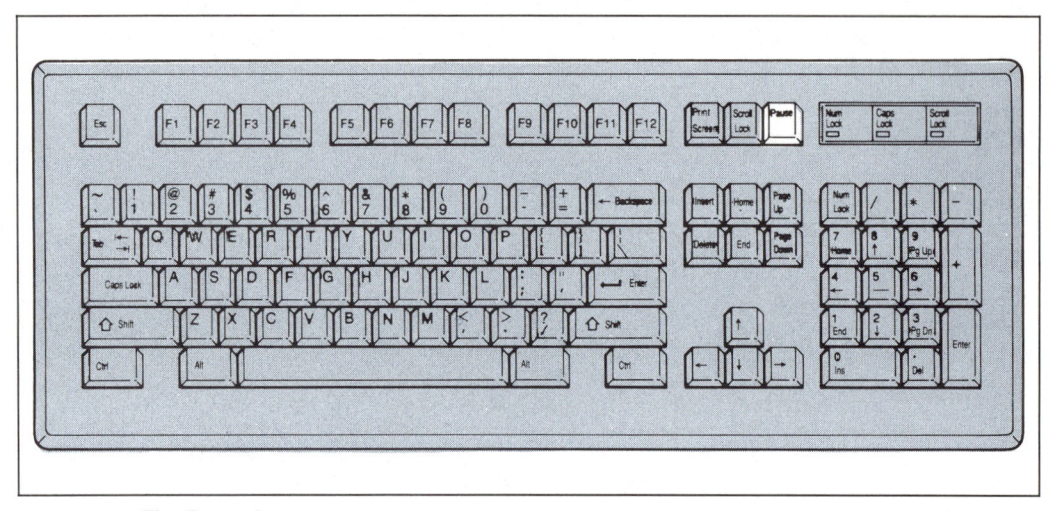

Figure 3.1: The Pause key

② As soon as the display starts to scroll up, press Pause the key to freeze the display on the screen. Too fast? Go back to step 1 and try again. (You can also hold down the Ctrl key and press S. Is this easier for you?)

③ When you are ready to start the display scrolling again, simply press any key. Now let's try using the DIR command with a parameter (that extra information you can use with commands).

④ You can use a file name as a parameter to display information about one particular file. For example, when you type

DIR COMMAND ↵

your PC displays the following on your screen:

```
COMMAND   COM   47845   04-09-91   5:00a
      1 file(s)   47845 bytes
           10964992 bytes free
```

If your version of DOS is different from ours, you may see a different date.

Upper- and Lowercase

With DOS (and many other operating systems), it does not matter whether you enter commands in uppercase (capital) letters or lowercase letters.

① Type the DIR command again, sometimes using the Shift key for uppercase letters and sometimes not; for example,

    Dir ↵
    DIR ↵
    dir ↵

You will see that the result is the same whether you enter the commands in lowercase or uppercase or a mixture of the two.

The Caps Lock Key

If you want to type in all capitals, you can use the Caps Lock key instead of having to hold down the ⇧ key. The Caps Lock key works only with the letters on your keyboard. You will still be able to type ; or / and you will still have to use the ⇧ key to type a % symbol.

The Caps Lock key is like an on/off key—press it once to type all capitals, and press it again to stop typing capitals. On some keyboards, the key does not stay down and there is nothing to indicate that you have pressed it, so you just have to remember. Whether you are using DOS commands or other software on your PC, the Caps Lock key works the same way.

Now enter some commands using the Caps Lock key.

① Press the Caps Lock key and type:

    DIR ↵
    DIR COMMAND ↵

These commands give the same results as before.

② When you have finished typing all capitals, press the Caps Lock key again to turn it off.

Canceling a Command

Suppose you typed DIR COMMEND instead of DIR COMMAND. How would you cancel the command so that you could enter it correctly?

You can cancel a command before you press ⏎ by holding down the Ctrl key and pressing the Break key (see Figure 3.2). The Break key cancels the command completely so long as you have not pressed ⏎. The computer will display ^C to tell you the command has been cancelled. You can then go on with whatever you meant to do.

Use the DIR command again to see how canceling a command works.

① Type

   DIR (Do not press ⏎)

② To cancel the command, hold down the Ctrl key and press the Break key.

That's enough about typed commands for now. Let's look at another way of telling your PC what to do.

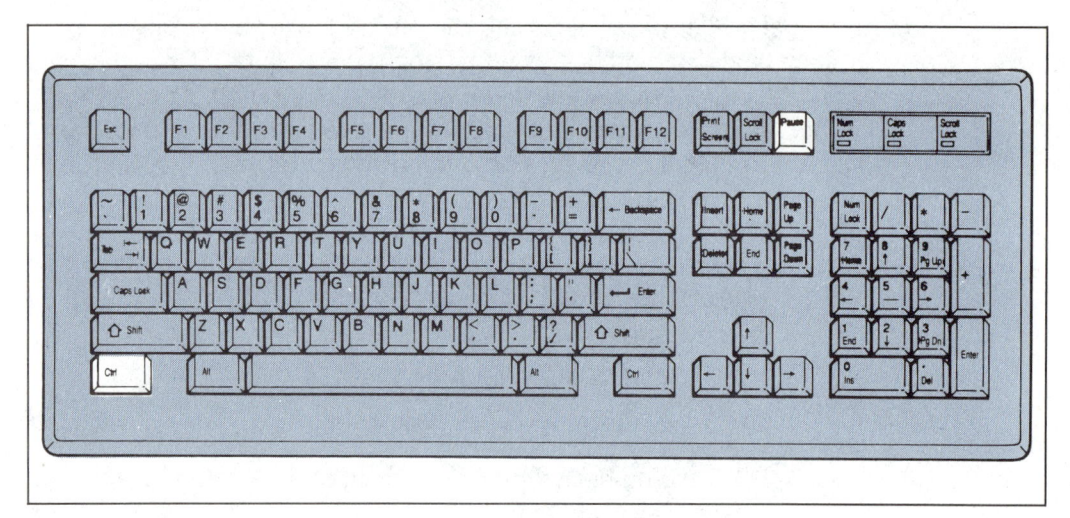

Figure 3.2: The Ctrl and Break keys

Choosing From Menus

Some software lets you perform functions by selecting them from several options displayed on a list called a *command menu*. A command menu is like a menu in a restaurant. It lists your choices and you select the one you want.

Software menus usually list the options with letters or numbers in front of them. You make your selection by typing the letter or number. Sometimes you select an option by typing the first letter of its name. If your PC has a mouse, you can use it to point at a menu choice and then press a button on the mouse to select that choice. Figure 3.3 shows a sample menu.

```
A- LOAD FILE
B- SAVE FILE
C- RENAME FILE
D - PRINT FILE
```

Figure 3.3: *A sample menu*

Using the menu in Figure 3.3, you would type A to load a file, B to name a file, and so on.

Software designers use menus rather than typed commands because they make the software easier to use. First of all, they eliminate lots of typing. The command or a description of a function is listed on the menu and you only have to type the letter or number that refers to the one you want. This helps people who are not used to using keyboards communicate with their computer.

The second reason designers use menus is that they make it easier for you to decide what you want by giving you a frame of reference. Also, you do not have to remember a lot of command formats because the menu reminds you how to give an instruction to your computer.

Want to try your hand with menus? We show you how to use menus in Chapter 7 with the spreadsheet program Lotus 1-2-3.

Using the Function Keys

Another way you can communicate with your computer is through function keys. As you know, the function keys are the row of keys at the top of the keyboard labeled F1 through F12. (On some keyboards the function keys are two rows of keys on the left of the keyboard.) You use these function keys with many software applications, so take a minute to get used to their layout.

When a software application program uses the function keys, it predefines each one of the keys to perform a specific operation. The function each key performs changes from application to application and can even change within a program.

At this point you are probably wondering *But how do I know which key does what when?* A very good question. Most programs that use function keys save you a lot of confusion by displaying the current meaning of the function keys on the screen, so you can tell which key to use. Others give you a template to place around the function keys on your keyboard. The template reminds you of each key's function.

We give you examples of how to use function keys when we introduce you to WordPerfect in Chapter 9.

Review

Three ways to tell your PC what to do:

- Type a command (a precise word or group of words).
- Choose a menu option by typing its letter or number. (If you have a mouse, point to the menu option and press a mouse button. Refer to your software documentation for instructions.)
- Choose one of the function keys (F1 through F12 on the keyboard) that corresponds to a screen label.

Use the DIR command to:

- List all files on the diskette.
- List a single file when you include the file name with the command.

To stop the display from scrolling out of view:

- Press pause (or Ctrl and S) to freeze the display.
- Press any key to start it again.

To type in capitals:

- The Shift Key (⇧) gives an uppercase letter or a symbol from the top row.
- The Caps Lock key gives all capitals; press it once for all capitals, press it again to end capitals.

To cancel a command:

- Hold down Ctrl and press Break.

Chapter 4

All about Diskettes

*F*eaturing

*Diskettes: types,
 handling, copying,
 formatting,
 write-protecting,
 storing, disk "space"*

Cleaning the drive

Without information that tells it how to work, your PC is useless. Normally, you keep the information that your PC needs on its hard disk. But how do you get it there in the first place? DOS and almost all applications are distributed on diskettes. You will often use diskettes to copy new information onto your hard disk and store copies of important information from your hard disk.

Diskettes are also known as *floppy disks* or *floppies*. They are called floppy because they bend easily. For this reason they have a protective covering that keeps them flat. The actual diskette on which information is stored spins inside this cover. Information is read from and written to the PC's memory by a read-Write head (similar to the playing arm on a record player) from the cut out area on the diskette.

Diskettes come in two sizes: 5 1/4-inch and 3 1/2-inch. The diskettes you use match the size of your diskette drives. Most PCs use 5 1/4-inch diskettes; however, many newer PCs use 3 1/2-inch diskettes.

It is not important that you understand how information is stored on a diskette; however, a couple of points can help you out on your first trip to your computer store. The type of diskette you choose must be compatible with your diskette drive.

First, information can be stored on one or both sides of a diskette. Diskettes that use only one side are called *single-sided* and those that use both sides are called *double-sided*. Most PC's use double-sided diskettes.

Second, the way information is stored on a diskette can vary. Some 5¼-inch diskettes (see Figure 4.1) are *single-density*, some are *double-density*, and others are *high-density*. Density simply refers to how the diskette stores characters as magnetic impulses. A double-density diskette can store twice as many characters (360 kilobytes) in the same amount of space as a single-density diskette. A high-density diskette can store four times as many characters (1.2 megabytes) as a double-density diskette.

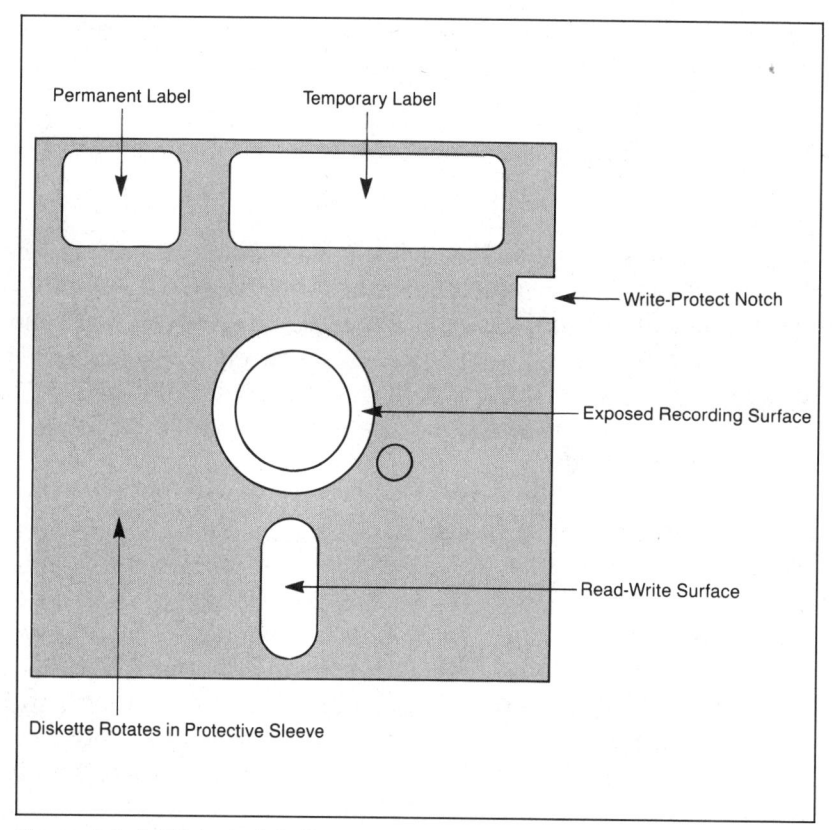

Figure 4.1: *A 5¼-inch diskette*

In this chapter, we will talk about how to handle, label, store, and copy your diskettes, but first of all, here are a few general rules to follow. These are the DON'Ts. They are here at the beginning so they are sure to catch your attention.

Rules for Handling Diskettes

- DON'T touch the exposed surfaces of a diskette.
- DON'T bend or fold a diskette.
- DON'T write on diskette labels with a sharp pencil or ballpoint pen.
- DON'T put diskettes near magnetized objects.
- DON'T put them in places that are very hot or very cold.
- DON'T let your diskettes get dusty.
- DON'T put diskettes near liquids and chemicals that may give off vapors.

What is the reason for all of these DON'Ts? Diskettes are like cassette tapes—you can record information on them and also play it back. Recording information is known as writing to the diskette; playing it back is known as reading the diskette. All of the things listed above can mar the surface of the diskette in such a way that your PC can no longer write or read information. A little carelessness and valuable information might be totally lost! If you take time to familiarize yourself with the DON'Ts now, you can save yourself a lot of aggravation later on.

The 3½-inch diskettes (see Figure 4.2) have a plastic jacket that protects the diskette from most of the dangers described above. A metal door covers the surface of the diskette for additional protection. The door slides open when the diskette is inside the drive, so that your PC can read information from and write information to the diskette. Even though 3½-inch diskettes have more protection, they are still vulnerable. To prevent losing any information, pay attention to our list of DON'Ts—no matter what kind of diskette you are using.

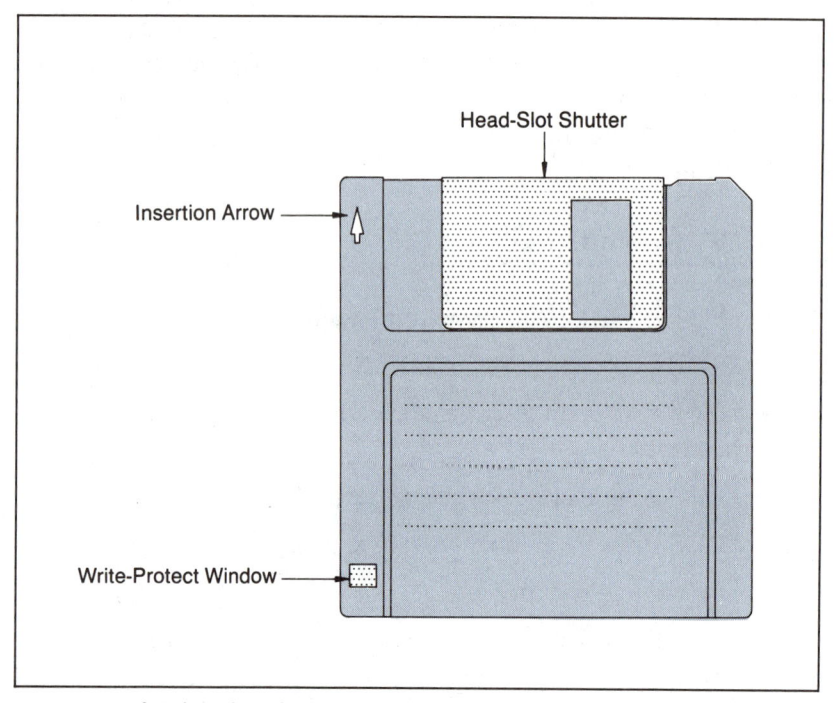

Figure 4.2: A 3½-inch diskette

Now we can talk about the DOs.

Labeling Diskettes

You will probably want to save related information on the same diskette, and it is useful to label each diskette with a general title. For example, if a diskette contains back-up copies of all of your reports for one sales region, an appropriate label is *Western Sales Region*. When pertinent, you might also include the date. Just as a book does not give all of its chapter titles on the cover, don't try to keep all the file names on the diskette label—the main subject is all you need. You can always get a complete file listing using the DIR command.

Diskette manufacturers provide sticky labels with each box of diskettes that you buy. Use them. Write the title on the label before you stick it on the diskette. If you want to change the title or write on the label after you have attached it to the diskette, use a felt-tip pen *only*. Ball-point pen and pencil are out—they can damage the diskette surface and make it unusable.

As shown in Figure 4.3, place the diskette label in the upper-right corner of the diskette next to the manufacturer's label (or in the upper part of a 3½-inch diskette). The labels are then all in one place for easy reference and storage. Be sure you do not put the label over any of the exposed surfaces—if you do, your PC will not be able to read from or write to the diskettes.

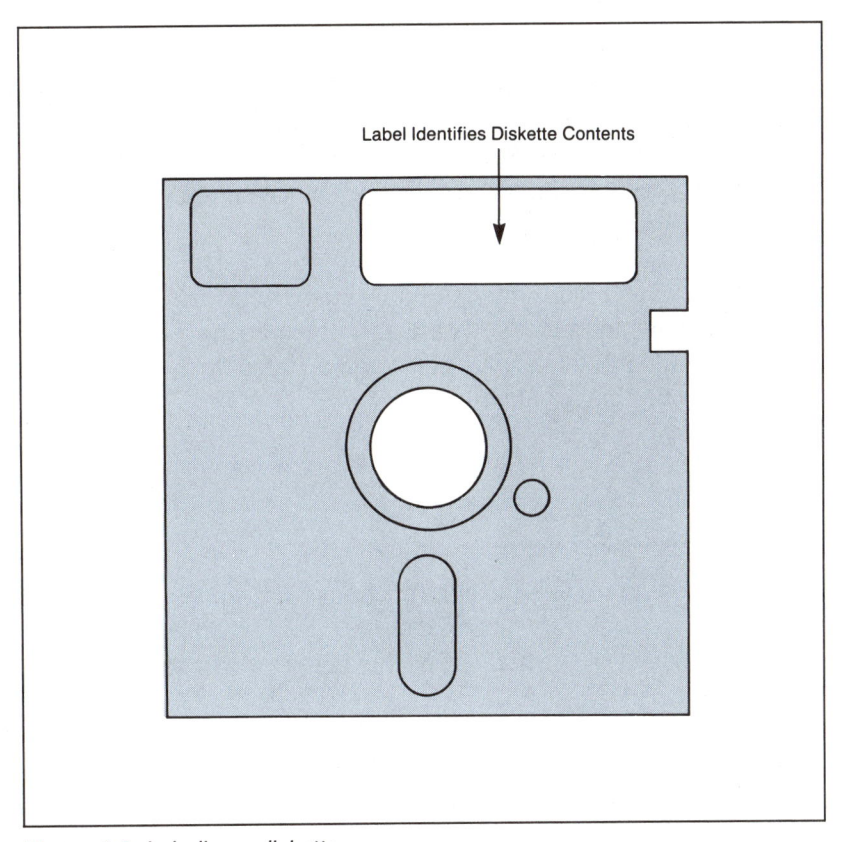

Figure 4.3: Labeling a diskette

Storing Diskettes

Store your diskettes in a safe, easily accessible place. As the number of applications that you use and the amount of information that you have stored on diskette increase, storage becomes more and more of a concern.

Many manufacturers package software the same way that IBM does, in a plastic sleeve that fits in the back of the application reference binder. You can store the software diskette there, or you may want to keep all of your applications together in a storage container. Several different kinds of diskette containers are available at computer stores or through other hardware and software vendors. Most offer some kind of filing divider and dust cover.

If you don't have a special diskette file, you can use the box you get when you buy diskettes. No matter how you store them, remember to use the paper sleeve they are delivered in. This protects them from dust and prevents you from accidentally touching the surface of the diskette.

Diskettes that contain highly sensitive or irreplaceable data should be stored even more carefully—under lock and key if necessary. Treat your computer software and stored documents just as you would any valuable document. In fact, go one step further and make a copy of any especially valuable diskettes.

Copying Diskettes

What if your computer malfunctions, or you delete something by mistake, or you simply lose a diskette? Things can go wrong, and they will. So get into the habit of backing up your software and information files.

Backing up means making a copy of the information stored on a diskette or hard disk. It protects you from losing information. You cannot appreciate the importance of adequate backup until you don't do it and wish you had. Most people don't bother at first, but sooner or later, they lose an important file. From that point on, they are always careful to make backup copies.

You can make a backup copy of all of the information on your hard disk, all information on a single diskette, or all information in a single file. You should develop your own backup procedure that includes all of these methods. Chapter 5 talks more about backing up in general. Right now, we are going to talk about copying an entire diskette, the procedure most useful for making backup copies of software programs. For example, you will want to make a copy of DOS.

Software manufacturers normally distribute applications on diskettes. You copy the program files from the diskettes to your hard disk, and use the hard disk version to run the program. The original diskettes are your backup. It is a good idea to copy the original diskettes as an extra precaution. You never know what might happen to them. (Some software manufacturers give you two copies of a program disk—one to copy to your hard disk and one for backup. Even if you have two disks, it is still a good idea to make a third.)

The manufacturers of some application software copy-protect their diskettes, which prevents you from copying them. However, you should always check your purchased software and make a backup copy if you can.

The DISKCOPY Command

Make a copy of the information on a diskette with the DISKCOPY command, which is part of DOS. DISKCOPY stands for *diskette copy*. You will need two diskettes: the diskette containing the information you want to copy, known to DOS as the *source diskette;* and a blank diskette, known to DOS as the *target diskette*, onto which the information will be copied.

The DISKCOPY command works only with diskette drives. You cannot use it to copy information to or from your hard disk. When you have just one diskette drive, you first copy information from the source diskette into the PC's memory, and then copy information from the PC's memory to the target diskette. The step-by-step procedure is outlined in the following list. If you have a two-drive system, you can copy information directly from one diskette to another. The procedure for using the DISKCOPY command with a two-drive system is explained in Appendix B.

① Insert the DOS operating diskette in the diskette drive and close the drive door.

② To begin copying the diskette, at the A> prompt type

DISKCOPY ⏎

③ Your PC displays the message:

Insert SOURCE diskette in drive A:

Press any key to continue ...

Since you have already inserted the diskette, press any key to begin the copy operation.

④ The red drive light goes on and you hear a whirring sound. When the information on the diskette has been transferred into memory, you will see

Insert TARGET diskette in drive A:

Press any key to continue ...

⑤ Remove the DOS diskette, and return it to its protective sleeve.

⑥ Insert a blank diskette in the drive, close the drive door, and press any key to copy DOS onto this diskette.

Depending on the amount of memory available in your PC, you may have to repeat steps 1 and 3 through 6 more than once. If this is the case, DOS will tell you when to change diskettes.

⑦ Remove the backup copy of DOS from the drive. Before you put it away, take time to label it. Write "Backup Copy of DOS operating disk" on a label and add the version number that is on the original DOS diskette. Peel off the label and place it in the top right corner of the diskette. Return the diskette to its protective sleeve, and keep it nearby; we'll use it later. Store the original diskette in a safe place.

Write-Protecting Diskettes

You need to be able to read all your diskettes, but you may not want to be able to write on some. For example, you probably will use the same diskettes over and over to back up important files. However you will not want to write on backup versions of application programs.

5¼-inch Diskettes

You can use a write-protect tab to prevent information from being added to or deleted from a 5¼-inch diskette.

Like labels, write-protect tabs are provided with diskettes when you buy them. They are small foil stickers that you place over the square notch on the side of the diskette. They are removable, so if you put a tab on a diskette to protect information that you do not want changed today, and tomorrow you decide that you want to change the information or overwrite the diskette, you can always take it off again.

Take a moment now to write-protect the copy of DOS that you made with the DISKCOPY command:

① Remove a foil write-protect tab from the sheet of tabs provided with your diskettes.

② Place the tab over the notch on the diskette as shown in Figure 4.4.

Now you are safe. No information can be added to or deleted from the diskette unless the tab is removed.

3½-inch Diskettes

3½-inch diskettes have write-protect tabs built in. You protect the diskette by sliding the tab toward the edge of the diskette as shown in Figure 4.5. When a 3½-inch disk is write-protected, you can see through the hole that the tab covers.

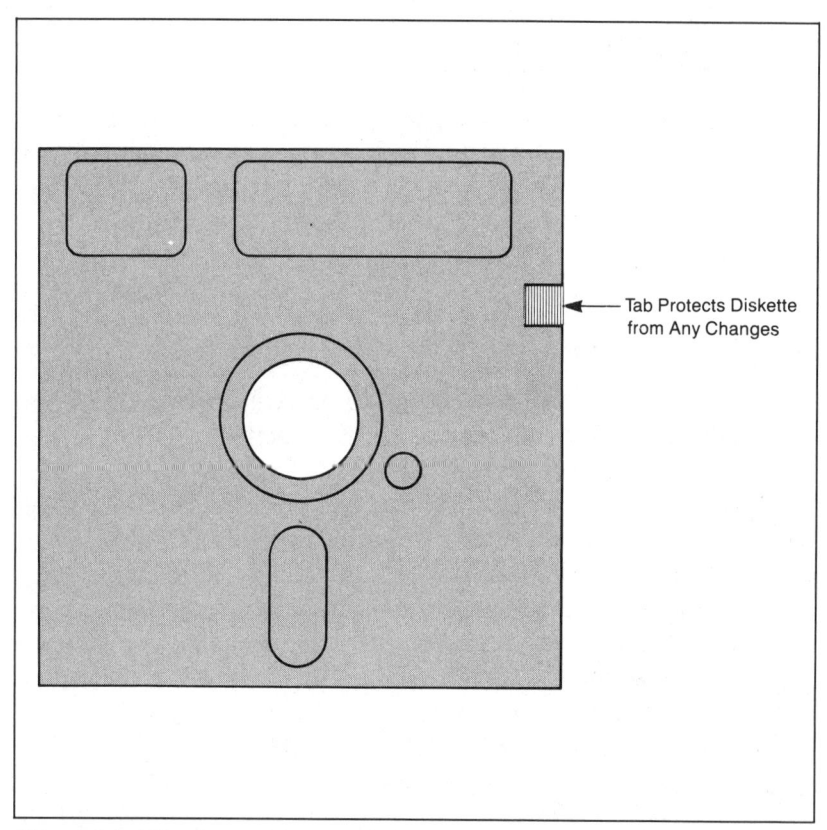

Figure 4.4: Write-Protecting a 5¼-inch diskette

Formatting a Diskette

When you *format* a diskette, you set the diskette to the recording format for DOS. Back to our stereo analogy again. If a record album has been recorded at 33 rpm and you play it back at 45 rpm, it sounds funny. Diskettes are somewhat the same except that they won't just sound funny; the computer won't be able to work with them at all. If the diskette has not been set to the format for DOS, you cannot even record information on it, let alone read it back.

Each operating system records information in its own format. When you format a diskette, you are indicating which format you are using. This means you do not have to buy different diskettes for different computers—you simply reformat and recycle them.

All about Diskettes   **57**

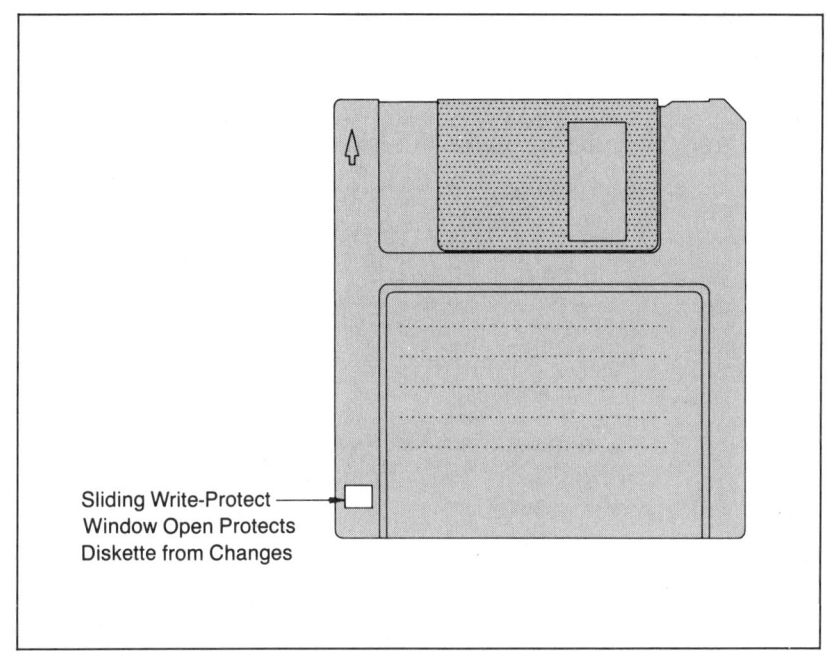

Sliding Write-Protect
Window Open Protects
Diskette from Changes

Figure 4.5: *Write-Protecting a 3½-inch diskette*

Formatting performs several operations: it sets the diskette to the correct recording format, checks the diskette for any defective areas that cannot receive information, and prepares the diskette to receive files. The result of all of this activity is a diskette that you can use to store information.

You did not need to format the diskette when you used the DISKCOPY command because your computer automatically formats the new diskette as part of that command. However, if you use a new diskette for any other purpose, you will have to use the FORMAT command first.

To format a diskette, use the FORMAT command followed by the drive identifier of the drive in which the new diskette is inserted. Take time to try it now.

① Insert a blank diskette in drive A:. Make sure you use a blank diskette because the format operation overwrites anything currently on the diskette.

FORMAT A: ⏎   *✱ SEE NEXT PAGE BEFORE ✱ DOING THIS*

> Whatever you do, don't forget the A:, or DOS will think you want to format your hard disk (C:) and will wipe out everything on it.

③ Your computer helps you out with this message:

**Insert new diskette for drive A:
and press ENTER when ready...**

Since you have already inserted the blank diskette, press any key to begin the formatting operation.

④ To let you know things are proceeding as planned, DOS sends you the message:

**Checking existing disk format.
Saving UNFORMAT information.
Verifying 360K.**

And when the operation is complete, it lets you know that, too:

**Format complete.
Volume label (11 characters, ENTER for none)?_**

**362496 bytes total disk space
362496 total bytes available on disk
    1024 bytes in each allocation unit.
     354 allocation units available on disk.**

Volume Serial Number is 2D38-OFD7

Format another (Y/N)?_

⑤ At this point you can remove the diskette from drive A, insert another, type Y and continue formatting, or you can simply type N.

Checking Diskette Storage Space

Information is stored on diskettes in bytes. You can think of one byte as the amount of space needed to store one character. It is a little more complicated than that, but that's pretty much all you need to know for now.

The memory of your computer and the storage capacity of your diskettes are measured in thousands of bytes (called kilobytes or K) or millions of bytes (called megabytes or MB). For example, a high-density 5¼-inch diskette has 1.2 megabytes, the equivalent of approximately 600 double-spaced printed pages.

When you first start working with your PC, you will be tempted to use a separate diskette for each file that you need to store. This is great for diskette manufacturers and dealers, but probably not the most efficient use of your diskettes. You may fall into this habit because you are nervous about running out of diskette space—it is impossible to tell how much information you have stored on a diskette by looking at it. But don't worry; DOS can help you out with the CHKDSK command, which tells you how much diskette space you have left. (CHKDSK stands for *check disk*.)

The CHKDSK Command

The CHKDSK command can help you manage your diskettes to full advantage. If you want to copy a program or report onto a diskette that already contains some information, you can use CHKDSK to find out if there is enough room.

Use your backup copy of DOS and practice checking diskette space by following these steps:

① Insert the diskette in drive A:, and close the drive door.

② Check the status of the diskette, including available space, by typing at the C> prompt

    CHKDSK A: ⏎

You receive a report that looks like this:

Volume Serial Number is 113C-ODE3

    362496   bytes total disk space
    319488   bytes in 32 user files
      43008   bytes available on disk

       1024   bytes in each allocation unit
        354   total allocation units on disk
        313   available allocation units on disk

```
   655360   total bytes memory
   601504   bytes free
```

As you can see, of the 362,496 bytes of storage on the diskette, 319,488 are used to store 32 files and 43,008 are available for storing additional information. (Your report will be slightly different.)

In addition, your computer tells you a bit about itself; of the 655,360 bytes of space in its memory, 53,856 are being used and hence 601,504 bytes are free. Those 53,856 bytes are taken up by DOS. (Again, the numbers for your PC will be different.) When you use an application program such as Lotus 1-2-3, you load that program into memory, too. The remaining memory is used as temporary storage for the reports or documents you are using with the application program.

③ You can also use the CHKDSK command to report the amount of space available on your hard disk. At the C> prompt, type:

CHKDSK ↵

You see a report that looks similar to the following one:

```
Volume MS-DOS_5   created 03-12-1991 2:43p
Volume Serial Number is 169D-6E19

  32010240   bytes total disk space
     49152   bytes in 3 hidden files
    157696   bytes in 72 directories
  17164288   bytes in 1036 user files
  14639104   bytes available on disk

      2048   bytes in each allocation unit
     16339   total allocation unit on disk
      5354   available allocation units on disk

    655360   total bytes memory
    601504   bytes free
```

This report is for a hard disk that has many files stored on it. Your hard disk probably has very few. It tells you that there are 32,010,240 bytes of storage on the disk. Of the available storage, 49,152 bytes are used to store hidden files; hidden files are files that

DOS alone uses. 157,696 bytes are used to store information about directories, which are described in Chapter 5. 17,164,288 bytes are used to store your files, and 14,639,104 bytes are available for storing new files.

Cleaning Diskette Drives

Diskette drives should be cleaned on a regular basis, depending on the amount of time you use your PC. Keeping the environment as free from dust as possible and cleaning your diskette drive are important maintenance steps.

The easiest way to clean the drives is with purchased cleaning kits which are available, with other computer supplies, at computer dealers. Each kit includes instructions for proper use, and usually either a pretreated fabric diskette or one that you treat with a cleaning solution. (Use only the cleaner provided in the kit.)

Turn on your PC, insert the cleaning diskette into the drive, and close the door. Leave it in for about a minute and then remove it. It's as simple as that!

Here is a quick review of this chapter; then we will tell you how to set up a filing system on your hard disk.

Review

Diskettes:

- Are used to store information.
- Can be written to and read from.
- Can be write-protected by covering the write notch with a special tab (5¼-inch diskettes) or by sliding the built-in tab toward the edge of the diskette (3½-inch diskettes).
- Must be handled with care.

When using diskettes:

- Label for easy reference.
- Store in a safe, dust-free spot.
- Back up all information.
- Do not write on the diskettes surface.

The DISKCOPY command:

- Copies all the information from one diskette to another.
- Does not copy to or from a hard disk.

The FORMAT command:

- Prepares a diskette for use.
- Warning: Never unintentionally format your hard disk.

The CHKDSK command:

- Checks the space on the diskette or hard disk in the designated drive.
- Displays a status report that includes the amount of free space on the disk and in the PC's memory.

Cleaning the diskette drives:

- Do on a regular basis depending on frequency of use.
- Use a purchased cleaning kit.

Chapter 5

Building a Filing System

*F*eaturing

Directories and subdirectories

Naming files

Wild card characters

Copying, erasing, renaming, and backing up files

All the information you store in your IBM PC is organized in files on your hard disk and on diskettes. As you acquire application programs and use them to create letters, reports, worksheets, and other documents, you will accumulate many files. In fact, you can store thousands of files on one hard disk. To keep track of all of these files, you can organize them into a filing system. Just as you organize paper files in folders in file cabinets, you organize your PC's files in directories on your hard disk.

If you think of your PC's hard disk as a filing cabinet, a *directory* is like a folder in that cabinet. It is a place for storing files that are related to each other in some way. For example, if you do word processing for several departments within your company, you might create a directory for each department. You would store the documents you create for a particular department in its directory. You use a directory's name as you might use a label on a folder to remind you what files are stored in it.

Diskettes can also have directories; however, because of the way that you use them and the amount of information you store on them, you rarely need to set up directories on diskettes. Throughout this chapter, we will assume that you are building a filing system on your hard disk.

Designing Your Filing System

DOS automatically creates the first directory on a hard disk or diskette for you. It is called the *root directory*, because, if you think of the directory structure as an inverted tree with many branches (see Figure 5.1), the first directory is like the root of the tree. All other directories branch off from it. You use the backslash (\) symbol to designate the root directory.

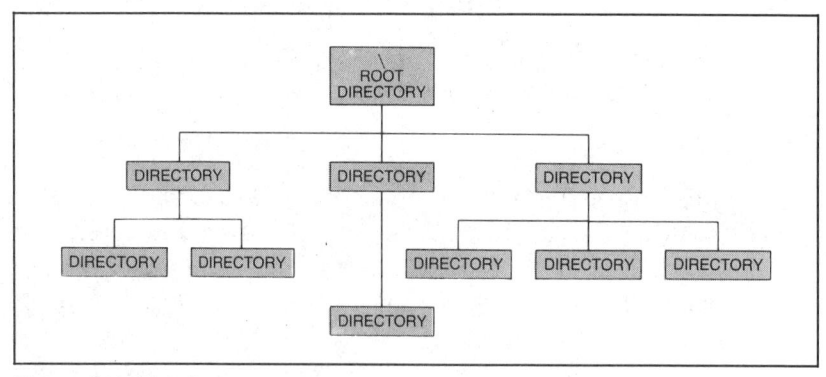

Figure 5.1: *The directory structure*

Within the root directory, you might create separate directories for different types of information. For example, you might have one directory in which you keep sales reports, one for sales plans, and one for expenses. Technically, these directories are called *subdirectories* because they exist within another directory (the root).

You can create as many subdirectories as you want within a directory, and directories can contain both files and subdirectories. For example, in the expenses directory, you might have a directory for each region. Within the directory for a particular region, you may keep a database file containing information about each salesperson and a directory for each salesperson that contains expense account files.

You can work in any directory you want. The directory in which you are working is called the *current directory*. Just as you can make drive C: or drive A: your current drive, you can make any directory your current directory. We will show you how to do this later in this chapter. From the current directory, you can work with files in any directory. We will also talk more about using files with commands later in this chapter.

Take some time now to start thinking about how you might organize your filing system. We will give you the commands to actually set up your filing system later in this chapter. Don't let your directory structure get so complicated that you can't remember where files are. If you do forget, use the DIR command to list the files in different directories until you find the file you want.

Most application programs recommend that you install them in their own directories. You may want to store information created with these programs in the application directories or in directories with names that are more meaningful to you. You can design your filing system in any way you want, and usually no two systems are the same. However, if other people will use your PC, you may want to consult them before you develop your system.

Assigning Directory Names

Each subdirectory within a directory is identified by a unique name. Whenever possible, choose names that reflect the information stored in the subdirectory. For example, SALESRPT is a good name for a sales report directory.

Rules for Directory Names

A directory name must be between one and eight characters long. It can consist of letters, numbers, or symbols. However, it must begin with a letter and cannot contain a period, asterisk, a question mark, a space, or any of the following symbols: < > : ; =] [.

Here are some directory names that follow the rules:

ACCTSPAY
LETTERS
BUDGETS
NEWSLTTR

Here are some names that are not allowed:

JAN.RPTS	(includes a period)
1988STMT	(begins with a number)
JOY WONG	(has a space)
FEBRECORDS	(exceeds eight characters)

Creating a Directory

Use the MKDIR command to create a new subdirectory. MKDIR stands for *make directory*. You type MKDIR and the directory's name.

The root directory is the current directory on drive C:. Let's create a subdirectory within it for storing example files.

① Make drive C: the current drive. After the A> prompt, type

C:↵

② Immediately after C>, type

MKDIR EXAMPLES ↵

In Chapter 3, you used the DIR command to list the files on the DOS diskette. DIR lists all of the files and subdirectories within a directory. Because the DOS diskette has only one directory, the root, you listed all the files on the diskette when you used DIR in Chapter 3. When the list you get from using the DIR command contains directories, DOS displays <DIR> after each directory name so that you can distinguish directories from files.

Now, use the DIR command to check for the new directory.

③ Immediately after C>, type

DIR ↵

You see a list of the files and directories in the root directory. In the list, you should see:

EXAMPLES <DIR> 04-09-91 12:01p

Figure 5.2 shows the directory structure for your hard disk.

```
         \
     ROOT
   DIRECTORY
        |
    EXAMPLES
```

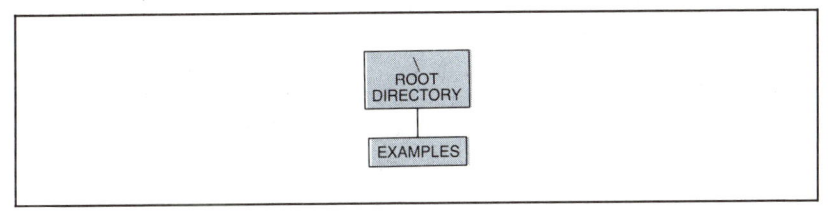

Figure 5.2: *Your hard disk's directory structure*

Changing the Current Directory

Your hard disk now has at least two directories: the root directory and the EXAMPLES directory you created. When you first start up your PC, the root directory is the current directory. The current directory is sometimes also called the *working directory* because it is the directory in which you are currently working.

You use the CHDIR command to change the current directory. CHDIR stands for *change directory*. You might change the current directory to an application directory before you use that application. The advantage of changing the current directory is that it is easier to work with files when they are in the current directory. We will say more about working with files later.

Practice changing the current directory.

① To make EXAMPLES the current directory, type

CHDIR EXAMPLES ⏎

② To learn which directory is the current directory, type

CHDIR ⏎

DOS tells you the name for the current directory:

C:\EXAMPLES

③ Now make a subdirectory within the EXAMPLES directory and name it SUB1. After the C>, type

MKDIR SUB1 ⏎

④ Let's make a second subdirectory and call it SUB2. After the C>, type

MKDIR SUB2 ⏎

Figure 5.3 shows the new directory structure for your PC.

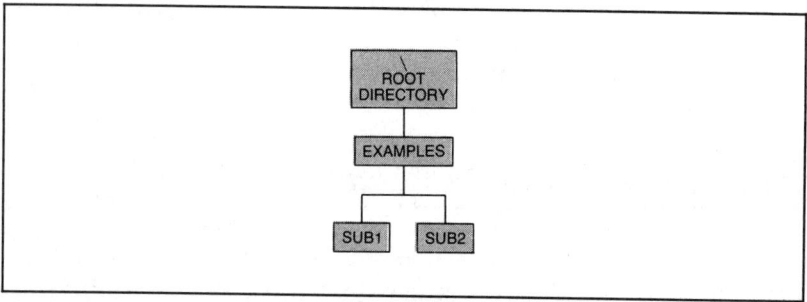

Figure 5.3: New directory structure

⑤ Make SUB1 the current directory. Type

CHDIR SUB1 ⏎

⑥ Now, check the current directory. Type

CHDIR ⏎

You should see:

C:\EXAMPLES\SUB1

But you named the new directory SUB1. What's all this other information DOS is giving you? DOS is telling you the *path name* for the directory. The path name tells you exactly where the directory belongs in your filing system. In this case, the path name tells you that the directory SUB1 is located in the EXAMPLES directory, which is located within the root directory on drive C:.

Using Path Names for Directories

You can think of a path name as a directory's full name. DOS uses path names to distinguish directories with similar names. You might use a person's full name in a similar way. For example, you might have a co-worker named Phillip Smith. Although you probably call him Phillip or Phil, in your company's employee records he is known by his full name, Phillip A. Smith. Using his full name distinguishes him from any other employees named Phillip or even Phillip Smith.

The DOS path name tells you exactly where the directory is located in your filing system. It includes the name of the drive on which the directory is located, the list of directories through which DOS must search to find the directory, and finally the directory name. A backslash character (\) separates each element of the path name. The backslash between the drive identifier and the first directory represents the root directory.

Figure 5.4 shows how you determine the path name for the directory SUB1.

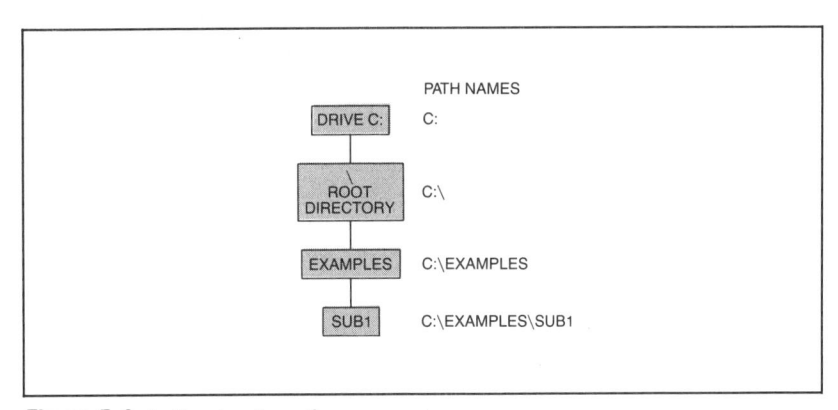

```
                    PATH NAMES
   DRIVE C:         C:
       \
     ROOT           C:\
   DIRECTORY
       |
    EXAMPLES        C:\EXAMPLES
       |
     SUB1           C:\EXAMPLES\SUB1
```

Figure 5.4: A directory's path name

You use a directory's path name with a command to tell DOS exactly which directory you want to use. You can always use the complete path name; however, there are two useful shortcuts:

- If the directory you want to use is on the current drive, you can leave the drive identifier out of the path name.

For example, since SUB1 is on the current drive, you can shorten its path name to the following:

\EXAMPLES\SUB1

- If the subdirectory is in the current directory, you can leave out all parts of the path name that tell DOS how to get to the current directory. You used this shortcut when you created the EXAMPLES directory.

You will find that using these shortcuts saves you a lot of typing. If you use one of the shortcuts and the command doesn't work as you expected, try the command again, but this time use the full path name.

Removing a Directory

When would you want to remove an entire directory? Suppose you set up a directory for information for a project. You might have several files in the directory. When the project is complete, you may no longer need to keep the files on your hard disk. You can copy the files to diskettes and delete the directory.

You use the RMDIR command to remove a directory. RMDIR stands for *remove directory*. You must remove all of the files from a directory before you can delete the directory. Before deleting files, you should always copy them to a diskette just in case you need them again sometime. We'll show you how to copy and delete files later in this chapter.

Let's remove one of the directories we created earlier.

① Type

RMDIR   \EXAMPLES\SUB2 ↵

You must type the path name because SUB2 is not a subdirectory within the current directory. However, because drive C: is the current drive, you do not need to include the drive identifier.(Remember, C:\EXAMPLES\SUB1 is the current directory.)

Building a Filing System   73

e SUB2 directory. Type

l of the directories and files
:ause EXAMPLES is not
ve its path name. Make

ganize your files. All of the
th the programs you use and
ist in files. We will spend the
vork with and back up files.

lentified by a unique name.
reflect the information stored
in the file. For example, _____ s probably the best name anyone could come up with for a file containing a product test plan. What if you forget the exact name of a file? Don't worry—you can always list all the files stored in a directory with the DIR command.

Rules for File Names

You normally assign a file name when you create the file in an application program or when you copy a file with DOS. File names follow the same rules as directory names. A file name must be between one and eight characters long. It can consist of letters, numbers, or symbols. However, it must begin with a letter and cannot contain a period, asterisk, a question mark, a space, or any of the following symbols: < > : ; =] [.

Obviously, as you accumulate more and more files, you will find it harder to come up with unique, meaningful names when you have only eight characters to play with. To overcome this problem, you have the option of tagging something called an *extension* onto the end of the file name. Extensions consist of a period followed by one to three characters. You can use them to identify the type of information in the file. For example, you could use the extension .LET to identify letters, or the extension .DOC for documents. If you give a file name an extension, you must include it any time you refer to the file.

Some application programs use extensions to distinguish different types of files, whereas program files are followed by an extension that identifies the language in which they are written. For example, the 1-2-3 spreadsheet program uses the extension .WK1 for spreadsheets and the extension .PIC for graphs. BASIC program files have the extension .BAS. These extensions are added automatically to the file name when you save the file. You do not have to enter them with the file name.

DOS also uses extensions to designate different types of files. For a complete description of DOS file extensions, refer to your DOS reference manual.

Here are some file names that obey the rules:

REGION3
SALESRPT.86
INCMSTMT.WK1
REDINC.LET

These files do not obey the rules:

1STFILE	(begins with a number)
MAIL LIST	(includes a space)
JONES ACCOUNT	(exceeds eight characters, includes a space)
MR.SMITH	(includes a period—SMITH is not a valid extension)

When you begin naming files, adopt some kind of a system. If most of your work is word processing, you may want to store all documents for a particular account in the same directory and follow a convention for naming letters, proposals, and project reports. If you frequently do reports with a spreadsheet program, you might want them all in one directory also, but since the directory would then include data for many clients, you would want to name the report files so that you could easily identify the client to which a particular report belongs.

Using Path Names for Files

Suppose you had organized your hard disk into directories for each of four sales regions and you were about to use a spreadsheet program to develop the sales plans for each region. Would you have to come up with a different file name for each sales plan? No. Because the files for the sales plans are in different directories, they can each have the same name—for example, SALESPLN.WK1. Figure 5.5 shows this file organization.

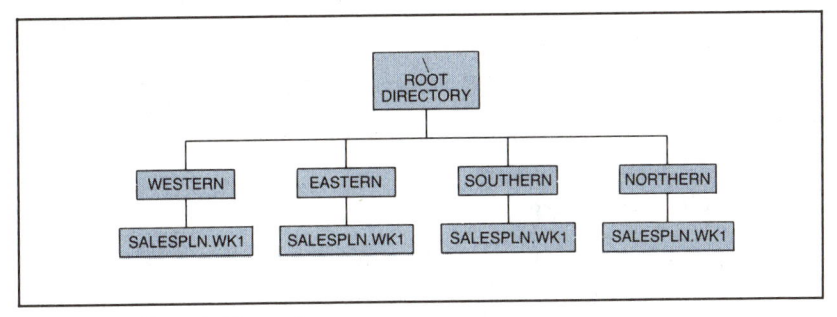

Figure 5.5: *Sample file system*

To DOS, the files are unique because they have different path names. Like a directory's path name, a file's path name tells its exact location in your file system. It includes the name of the drive on which the file is located, the list of directories through which DOS must search to find the file, and finally the file name. A backslash character (\) separates each element of the path name. The backslash between the drive name and the first directory represents the root directory. The path names for the sales plans in the example would be

    C:\WESTERN\SALESPLN.WK1
    C:\EASTERN\SALESPLN.WK1
    C:\SOUTHERN\SALESPLN.WK1
    C:\NORTHERN\SALESPLN.WK1

You can see that each path name is unique. You use path names with commands to tell DOS exactly which file or directory you want to use. You can use the same shortcuts that you use for directory path names for file path names:

- If the file you want to name is on the current drive, you can leave the drive name out of the path name.
- If the file is in the current directory, you can leave out all parts of the path name that tell DOS how to get to the current directory.

If you request a file without giving DOS enough information to find it, you receive the message

File not found

All you need to do is retype the command using the file's complete path name.

Wild Card Characters

In a card game, a wild card can represent any card in the deck. DOS has two wild card characters, the asterisk (*) and the question mark (?). An * in a file name or extension means that any character can fill that position and any remaining positions in the name or extension. A ? in a file name or extension means that any character can fill that position only.

Once you start to build a system of directories containing many files, you will find wild card characters an easy way to work with groups of file names. For example, you can list a group of files, perhaps all files with the letter M, or all files with the extension .BAS.

Here's how wild card characters work.

① Insert the duplicate DOS operating diskette that you made in Chapter 4 in drive A:. (We use the DOS diskette for our examples because we don't know exactly which files you have on your hard disk.)

② Use * to list all files on the DOS diskette beginning with M. Immediately after C>, type

DIR A:M* ⏎

Your PC lists the files on the DOS diskette that begin with M. (Our version of DOS has two files that begin with M; yours may have more.)

③ To list all files with the extension .EXE, type

DIR A:*.EXE ↵

If your copy of DOS is the same as ours, this command lists 43 files, all with the extension .EXE.

④ Try using a ? to list all files that are named BASIC or BASIC followed by another character. Type

DIR A:?BASIC ↵

Two file names are listed on our copy of DOS:

QBASIC   HLP
QBASIC   EXE

If there were a file named BASICA on the DOS diskette, it would not be listed with the ?—you would have to use * immediately after the name BASIC.

Copying Files

You have already used the DISKCOPY command to copy an entire diskette. Often you will want to copy only a single file or group of files, not the whole diskette. That is what the COPY command is for. When you copy a file, you do just that—copy it. It is like using your office copier. The original remains intact, but you now have a duplicate.

Making a Copy on Another Disk

Why would you copy a file from one disk to another? One reason is to back up your work. Making a copy of a file on a second disk means you have a duplicate of the file for safety. Normally, you back up files on your hard disk by copying them to a diskette. There are also lots of other reasons for copying files from one disk to another. Most software manufacturers distribute application programs on diskettes. Since you will want to keep all of your applications on your hard disk, you must copy the program from the diskette to the hard disk. (The process of installing an application on your hard disk may involve more than just copying files; be sure to follow the software manufacturer's instructions.) You may also use diskettes to share information with co-workers. For example, a co-worker might give you a diskette containing standard letters for responding to different customer requests. Before you modify these letters for particular customers, you may want to copy them to your hard disk.

We will assume that you still have the duplicate DOS diskette in drive A: and that C:\EXAMPLES\SUB1 is the current directory. We are going to copy the file TREE.COM from the diskette in drive A: to a new file called OAK.COM in the current directory:

① Immediately after C>, type

COPY A:TREE.COM OAK.COM ↵

You do not need to include a path for the duplicate file because you are copying it to the current directory. Because you are giving it a new name, you must supply the name and the extension.

When it has finished the copying operation, DOS gives you the message:

1 File(s) copied

② Now let's copy TREE.COM from DOS in drive A: to a new file with the same name in the current directory of drive C:. Immediately after C>, type:

COPY A:TREE.COM ↵

You must give the full path name for the file on drive A:. Because you want the copy in the current directory to have the same name as the original, you do not have to give DOS a new name. When copying is complete, you will see the same message as before on your screen.

③ Want to try an example with wild card characters? To copy all files beginning with the letter R from the diskette in drive A: to the EXAMPLES directory on drive C:, type

COPY A:R*.* C:\EXAMPLES ↵

Something new happens here. When you use wild cards to copy multiple files, DOS lists the name of each file as it copies them so that you know what you are getting. At the end of the copy operation, the message on your screen looks like this:

**RECOVER.COM
REPLACE.EXE
RESTORE.COM
3 File(s) copied**

When you use the * wild card in this way, you need to type an * for the file extension as well as the file name. Typing COPY R* would not have copied any files, since all files beginning with R on the DOS diskette have extensions. Remember, when a file has an extension, you must use it whenever you use the file name.

Making a Copy in Another Directory

Suppose you keep all the documents related to each of your clients in separate directories. You need to write a letter to Mr. Jones and you remember that last month you wrote a similar letter to Ms. Smith. Instead of typing the letter all over again, you can copy the letter from Ms. Smith's directory to Mr. Jones' directory and make whatever changes are necessary, thereby saving yourself a lot of typing.

Let's practice copying a file from one directory to another by copying TREE.COM from C:\EXAMPLES\SUB1 to C:EXAMPLES. We are assuming that C:\EXAMPLES\SUB1 is still your current directory.

① Immediately after C>, type

COPY TREE.COM \EXAMPLES ←

You do not have to include the full path name for the original file because it is in the current directory. Because you are using the same file name, you do not have to give a name for the duplicate in the EXAMPLES directory.

② Now copy TREE.COM from the EXAMPLES directory to a file called WILLOW in the current directory. Type

COPY \EXAMPLES\TREE.COM WILLOW ←

You have to give DOS the full path name for the original file because it is not in the current directory. You give a new name only for the duplicate file. Its path is not required because you are copying it to the current directory.

Making a Copy in the Same Directory

Suppose you produce a monthly report. Instead of redoing the whole report each month, you can simply make a copy of last month's report, update the copy in a few places, and store it as this month's report. If you used the original rather than a copy, you would no longer have a report for last month!

When you copy a file within a directory, you must give the copy a different file name—DOS will not let you have more than one file with the same name in a directory. So, for example, the copy of a file named SALESRPT might be called SALESRPT.CPY.

If you want to copy a file in the current drive and directory, you do not need to give the drive name and directory name in the path name. You simply give the name of the original file followed by a space and the name of the duplicate file.

Let's try making a copy of the file WILLOW in the current directory. We will call the copy PINE.

Type

COPY WILLOW PINE ⏎

You see the message:

1 File(s) copied

If you need proof that your PC did as you asked, check the directory by typing

DIR ⏎

There should now be a file named PINE at the end of the list.

At this point, remove the DOS diskette from drive A: and store it in a safe place.

Renaming a File

What if you think of a better name for a file, or want to change the name to be consistent with other file names? You can always change the name of a file with the RENAME command. You give the current name of the file and the name you want to change it to. It's that simple. The next time you want to look for the file, use its new name. Nothing in the file will change—only the name will be different.

In an earlier exercise, we copied the file TREE.COM from the DOS diskette in drive A: to the current directory on drive C: (C:\EXAMPLES\SUB1). We called the copy OAK. Now we have decided that the name OAK is not descriptive enough and that the name NEWTREE would suit us better. Let's rename the file.

① Immediately after C>, type

RENAME OAK NEWTREE ⏎

② DOS does not give you any message to confirm the change, but you can check that things went smoothly with the DIR command. Type

DIR ⏎

There should now be a file called NEWTREE in the SUB1 directory. If OAK had been in a directory other than the current directory, you would have had to use its full path name to identify it.

Erasing or Deleting a File

If you no longer need a file, you can delete it with either the ERASE command or the DEL command. Both do the same thing. The important thing to remember with these commands is that once a file has been deleted, it is gone; so be sure you know what the file contains before you delete it.

All you need to do to delete a file is give the command followed by the path name. As always, the path name includes the drive identifier, the necessary directory names, and an extension when they apply.

① Let's delete the file NEWTREE in the current directory of drive C:. Immediately after C>, type

DEL NEWTREE ⏎

Since NEWTREE is in the current directory, we need only type the file name.

② Use the DIR command to check that the file has been deleted.

③ Earlier on we created a file named PINE in the current directory. Let's erase that file now. Immediately after C>, type

ERASE PINE ↵

④ Are you ready to use the wild card character * to delete a couple of files at once? If you remember, we still have copies of the DOS files RECOVER.COM, REPLACE.EXE, and RESTORE.COM in the EXAMPLES directory. Delete them by typing immediately after the C>:

DEL \EXAMPLES R*.* ↵

Be very careful when using * to erase files. You do not want to lose more than you planned. You could in fact delete all the files in a directory by typing the ERASE or DEL command with *.*. In response, DOS would give you the opportunity for second thoughts by asking: **Are you sure (Y/N)?** If you know what you are doing, type Y; if not, you can cancel the operation by typing N.

Let's delete all the files in the two directories, EXAMPLES and SUB1, that we created earlier.

① Type

CHDIR \ ↵

② Next delete all of the files in the SUB1 directory. Type

DEL EXAMPLES\SUB1\ *.* ↵

③ DOS asks you if you are sure you want to delete all of the files in a directory. Type Y. If you wanted to cancel the command, you would type N.

④ Now delete the files in the EXAMPLES directory. Type

ERASE EXAMPLES*.* ↵

⑤ When DOS asks if you are sure you want to delete all of the files in the directory, type Y.

⑥ Type

    DIR ⏎

Backing Up Your File System

Backing up your file system means making a copy of the information stored on your hard disk. You will invest a lot of time in installing application programs, setting up directories, and creating files on your hard disk. You can protect a single file by copying it onto a diskette, but the only way you can protect all of your files and your directory structure is by backing up your hard disk. Backing up your disk regularly protects you from wasting your effort and losing your information.

You should begin by establishing a regular schedule for performing complete and incremental backups. A complete backup copies all of the directories and files on your hard disk. If you have a lot of information stored in your file system, a complete backup can take a long time. An incremental backup copies the directories and files that have changed since the last complete backup.

How often you should perform a complete backup depends on how often you use your PC and how important your files are. For most people, weekly complete backups with daily incremental backups are adequate. Others may not need to perform backups as often. People who use their PC heavily may want to perform a complete backup every day.

Backup Methods

There are several ways to perform backups. You can choose from several forms of backup media. You might use diskettes, tape cartridges, or cartridge disks. To use any media other than diskettes, however, you must purchase additional hardware. DOS gives you commands for backing up to diskettes and tape. There are also backup programs available from software manufacturers. These programs can be faster and easier to use than DOS commands. We will describe how to back up your hard disk using DOS commands and diskettes since these methods are available to all PC owners. This method can be very time-consuming compared to using other media and other programs; therefore, we recommend that you investigate other options if you have a lot of files to back up.

Using the Backup Command

To perform a complete backup of your hard disk,

① Change your current directory to the root directory. After C>, type

CHDIR \\ ⏎

② Use the BACKUP command to tell DOS to back up all files in the current directory and all of its subdirectories from drive C: to drive A:. After the C>, type

BACKUP C: A:/S ⏎

You see the following message:

Insert backup diskette 01 in drive A:
Warning! Files in the target drive
A:\\ root directory will be erased
Strike any key when ready

③ Insert a formatted diskette in drive A:. Be sure to use a disk that does not contain any valuable information. Press any key. DOS begins backing up files. You see the following message:

*** Backing up files to drive A: ***
Diskette Number: 01

DOS lists the path name for each file it backs up. This is a good time to take a coffee break or make a few phone calls. It can take 15 to 20 minutes to fill a diskette. When the first

Building a Filing System

diskette is full, you see the following message:

**Insert backup diskette 02 in drive A:
Warning! Files in the target drive
A:\ root directory will be erased
Strike any key when ready**

④ Remove the first diskette from drive A:. Write BACKUP DISKETTE 1 and the date on a label, and place the label on the diskette. It is important to label and number your backup diskettes. If you need to restore files to your system from them, you must use them in order.

⑤ Insert a new diskette in drive A: and press any key to continue the backup. DOS tells you that it is continuing with the backup and lists the files backed up.

⑥ When the second diskette is full, label it and insert a new one. Continue following DOS's instructions to insert new diskettes until the backup is complete. You know that the backup is complete when you see the C> prompt.

You can also use the BACKUP command to back up only those files that have changed since the last complete backup.

① Change your current directory to the root directory. After C>, type

CHDIR \ ↵

② Use the /S and /M parameters with the BACKUP command. After the C>, type

BACKUP C: A:/S/M ↵

The /M at the end of this command tells DOS to back up only the files that have changed since the last backup. It backs up all files in the current directory and all of its subdirectories from drive C: to drive A:. You see the following message:

**Insert backup diskette 01 in drive A:
Warning! Files in the target drive
A:\ root directory will be erased
Strike any key when ready**

③ Insert a formatted diskette in drive A:. Be sure to use a disk that does not contain any valuable information. Press any key. DOS begins backing up files. You see the following message:

*** Backing up files to drive A: ***
Diskette Number: 01

DOS lists the path name for each file it backs up.

④ If necessary, insert additional disks when DOS asks for them. Be sure to label each disk with its number, the date, and INCREMENTAL BACKUP. When the backup is complete, you see the C> prompt.

Using the RESTORE Command

We hope you will never have to use your backup files. However, things can go wrong. For example, you might accidentally delete an important file. You use the RESTORE command to copy files from your backup diskettes to your hard disk. We show you how to restore files in this chapter. Because you do not need to restore files at the moment, just read through the procedure now. Reread it when you actually need to restore files.

① Find the diskettes from your last complete backup.

② With the RESTORE command, you give DOS the complete path names for the files you want to RESTORE. Of course, you can also use wild card characters. Let's assume that you accidentally deleted all the files in a directory named NEWACCTS, and now you want to copy them from your backup diskettes. You would type

RESTORE A: C:\NEWACCTS *.* ↵

This command tells DOS to restore all files in the NEWACCT directory from drive A: to drive C:. You see the following message:

Insert backup diskette 01 in drive A:
Strike any key when ready

③ Insert the first backup diskette in drive A:, then press any key. You must copy files from the backup diskettes in order. You see another message:

* * * Files were backed up 03/03/89 * * *
* * Restoring files from drive A: * * *

DOS lists the names of the files as it restores them. When it completes restoring the files from the first backup diskette or if it does not find the files you want on the first diskette, DOS asks you to insert the second diskette.

④ Continue to insert the backup diskettes into drive A: as DOS asks for them. The restoration is complete when you see the C> prompt.

⑤ Now restore the files from your last incremental backup. Follow the procedure in steps 1 through 4, but use the diskettes from the incremental backup. DOS will only replace the files on the incremental backup disks.

In this chapter, we have covered a lot of information that you will use on a regular basis. So here is a quick review to refer back to as you begin using your PC on your own.

Review

Filing system:

- Consists of directories and files.
- DOS creates the first directory, called the *root*, automatically.
- The \ symbol designates the root directory.
- A directory can have any number of *subdirectories*, and its subdirectories can have their own subdirectories.

Directory and subdirectory names:

- Each subdirectory within a directory must have a unique name.
- Directory names can be one to eight characters long and must begin with a letter.
- Directory names cannot include a period, space, asterisk, or question mark.

Path names:

- You must use path names with commands to tell DOS exactly which file or directory you want to use.
- The path name for a file consists of its drive identifier, a \ for the root directory, a list of all of the directories through which DOS much search to find the file with directory names separated by a \, and the file name including the extension.
- The path name for a directory consists of its drive identifier, a \ for the root directory, a list of all of the directories through which DOS much search to find the file with directory names separated by a \, and the name of the directory you want to use.
- When the file or directory you want to use is on the current disk, you can omit the drive identifier from the path name.
- When the file or directory you want to use is in the current directory or one of its subdirectories, you can omit all of the information in the path name that tells DOS how to get to the current directory.

The MKDIR command:

- Creates a new directory.

The CHDIR command:

- Changes the current directory to the directory you name.

- Reports the name of the current directory if you don't name a directory.

The RMDIR command:

- Removes a directory from your disk.
- Only works if you first delete all files from the directory.

File names:

- Each file in a subdirectory must have a unique name.
- A file name can be one to eight characters long and must begin with a letter.
- You cannot include a period, space, asterisk, or question mark in a file name.

File extensions:

- A file extension is a three-character identifier separated from the file name by a period. (It can be less than three characters, but not more.)
- If a file name has an extension, you must include the extension when you use the file name.

Wild card characters:

- An asterisk in a file name or extension means that any character can fill that position and any remaining positions in the name.
- A question mark in a file name or extension means that any single character can fill that position only.

The COPY command:

- Is used to make a copy of a file on another disk, in another directory, or in the same directory. You can give the copy either the same name as the original or a new name.

- Can be used with wild card characters to copy several files at once.

The RENAME command:

- Renames a file.

The DEL or ERASE command:

- Deletes a file.

Backing up your hard disk:

- Saves the information and effort in your file system.
- Requires a regular schedule of complete and incremental backups.
- Is accomplished with any of a variety of backup media and backup programs.
- Use the BACKUP command to perform backups to diskette.
- Use the RESTORE command to copy files from backup diskettes to your hard disk.

Part III

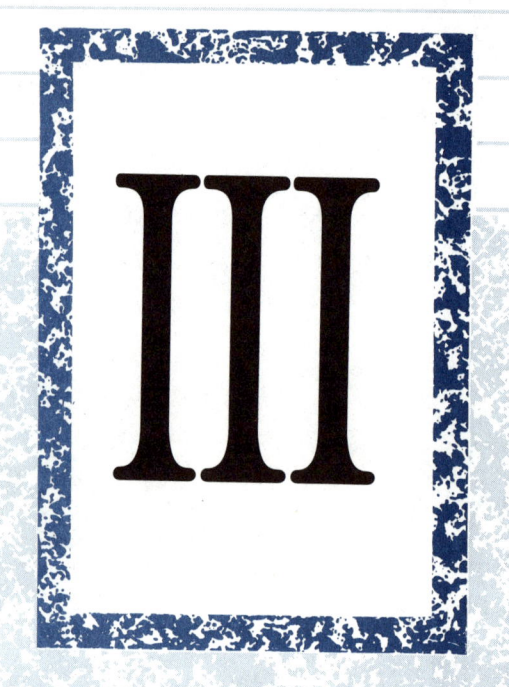

Using Operating Environments

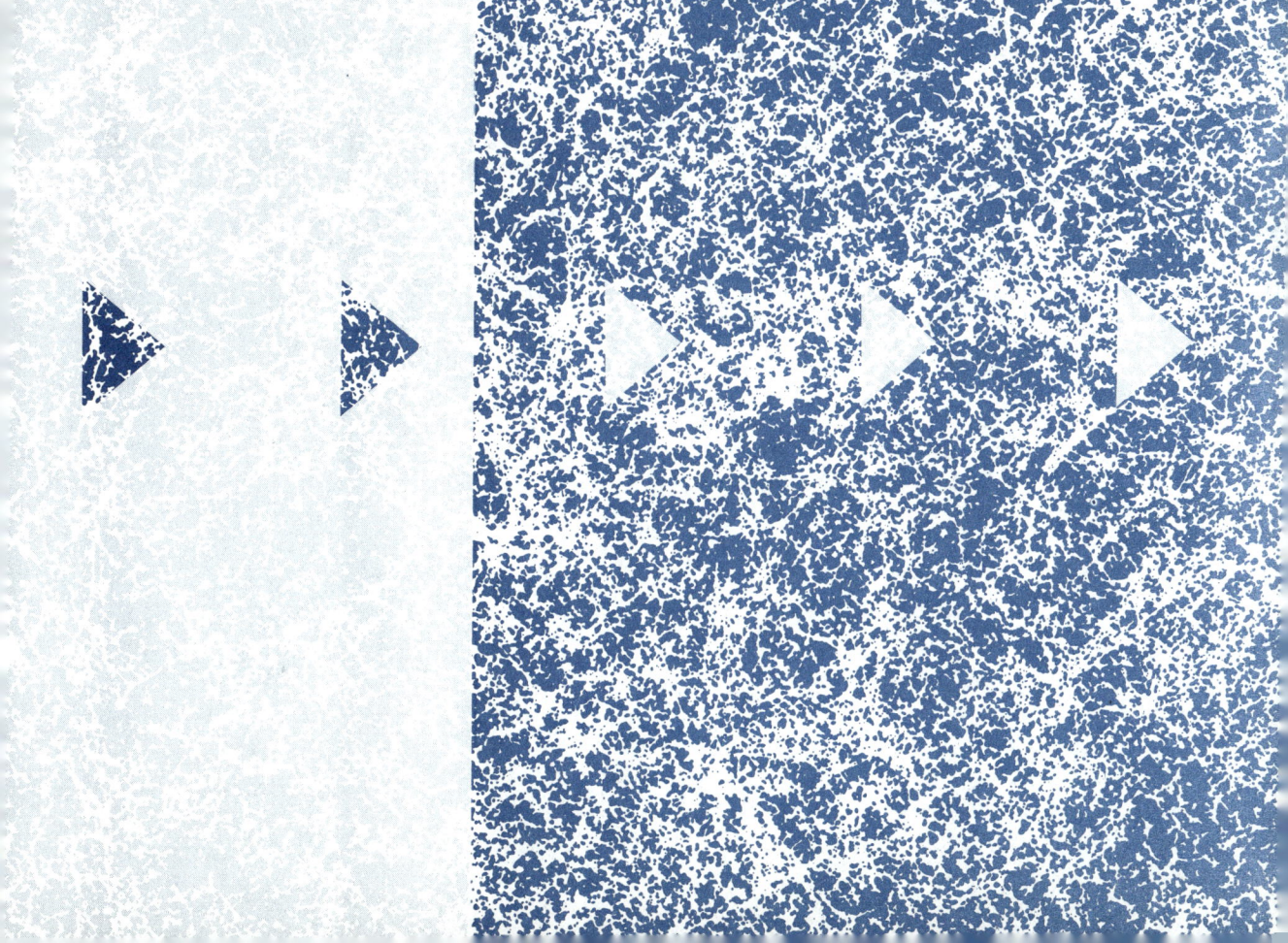

Chapter 6

Using the DOS 5 Shell

*F*eaturing

Using the Mouse or the Keyboard to pull down menus and execute commands
Selecting and Changing Views

The disk operating system (DOS) on your PC coordinates the various functions of the computer's software and hardware. DOS lets you communicate with your system so that information is entered, processed and stored according to your instructions.

DOS Version 5 comes with the Shell, a graphical interface that simplifies your interaction with the computer. It lets you easily organize files and directories, run programs, and execute most DOS commands. The Shell also lets you run multiple programs simultaneously, so you can switch easily between programs.

This chapter gives you basic instructions for using the Shell. It contains an explanation of the Shell's main elements and takes you through a series of exercises. When you have finished the chapter, you will have a general understanding of the Shell's operation and can begin using it to work with your operating system and other programs.

We assume that you have already installed DOS on your computer. You should refer to the DOS documentation for installation instructions.

Loading the Shell

The Shell might appear automatically when you start your computer. If not, the first step is to start the Shell. At the command prompt, type

dosshell

then press ←. The DOS Shell appears on your screen.

The DOS Shell

The first time that you start the Shell, the view displays the directories, files, and programs on your hard disk drive (see Figure 6.1).

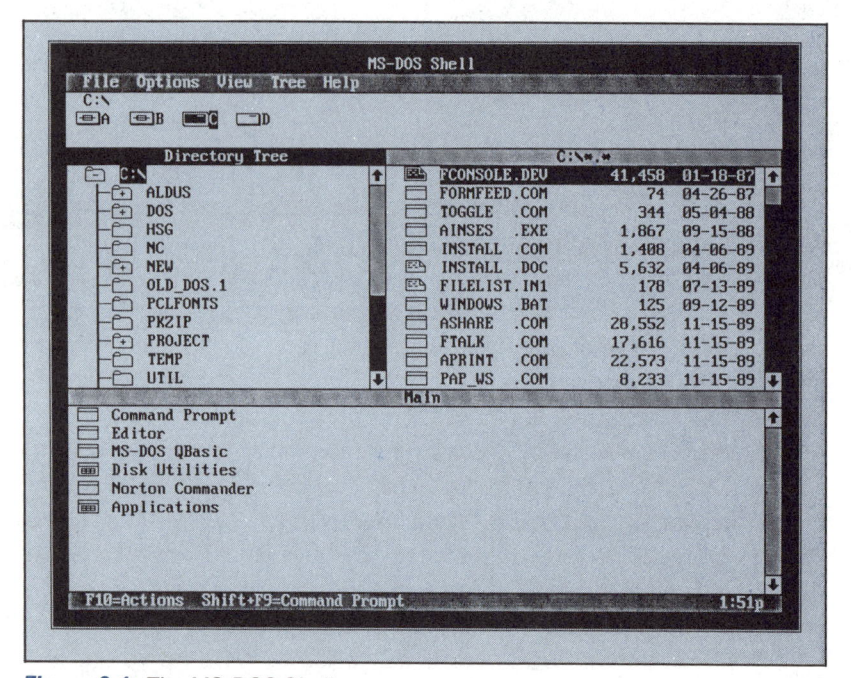

Figure 6.1: The MS-DOS Shell

The Shell display is divided into several areas. To use the Shell, you need to know the names and uses of these areas. The following list gives you a brief explanation of the basic Shell elements.

- The title bars identify each area.

- The menu bar lists the available menus. It contains the **File, Options, View, Tree,** and **Help** menus. Each of these menus contains commands that you can execute in the DOS Shell.

- The drive letters and icons display the available drives on your computer. The view probably displays the A drive (your floppy disk drive) and the current hard disk drive that is active. Depending on the configuration of your system, additional drives may be displayed.

- The active drive is highlighted and also identified by the drive letter above the icons.

- The directory tree displays the available directories on your hard disk drive. The current tree displays the root directory and all first-level directories on your hard disk drive. You can select and manipulate directories and subdirectories in this area.

- The file area displays the files in the selected directory. The title bar for the file area contains the path for the displayed files. You can organize and run files displayed in this area. The current view displays files in the root directory.

- The program area displays the available program groups and program items. You can run files in these groups, and you can add new items and groups to the area.

- The scroll bars are the bars and arrows at the side of each area. You can use the scroll bars to move through a long list and view all of the items.

- The selection cursor highlights a selected item or area. It is indicated by a bar of different intensity (or color, if you have a color monitor).

- The status line, at the bottom of the Shell, displays the time, any Shell messages, and helpful shortcut keys that you can use.

Executing Commands in the DOS Shell

To use the Shell elements listed previously, you need to be familiar with the basic tools of your PC, the keyboard and the mouse (if your computer has a mouse).

You can use the mouse and the keyboard independently or in combination. In the beginning exercises, we provide instructions for using both tools. As you work through the chapter and become more familiar with the Shell, the instructions are less specific, and you can choose which tool to use.

If you have a mouse on your PC, you can see the mouse pointer icon on the Shell display. You can use the mouse to select items or execute commands. When you move the mouse on a flat surface, the pointer moves on the screen. To select an item, move the mouse until the pointer is touching it, then click the mouse button once or twice, depending on the task. You can also move an item by pointing to it, holding down the mouse button, and dragging the item to its new destination.

When you use your PC's keyboard, you use the function keys and the Alt, Ctrl, Shift, and Tab keys to execute commands. You can use these keys alone or in combination.

You should practice using the mouse and keyboard to execute menu commands.

Using the Mouse with Menus

To open the Shell Basics help window, follow these steps:

① Move the mouse until the mouse pointer rests on the Help menu.

② Click the mouse button once. The Help menu commands are displayed.

③ Click the Shell Basics command. The MS-DOS Shell Basics window opens, displaying a list of topics from which you can select.

④ To close the window, click the OK button.

*U*sing the Keyboard with Menus

To open the MS-DOS Shell Basics help window, follow these steps:

① Press Alt to select the menu bar.

NOTE: Each menu name and command has one letter underlined. To open the menu or execute the command, press the appropriate letter key.

② Press H to display the Help menu.

③ Press S to select the Shell Basics command. The MS-DOS Shell Basics window opens, displaying information about using the DOS Shell.

④ To close the window, press ⏎.

Now that you are familiar with the basic elements of a DOS Shell, you're ready to learn how to use the Shell for organizing your files and running your programs.

*C*hanging the View in the DOS Shell

As we said earlier, the current Shell view displays the files and programs available on your hard disk drive. The Shell offers several display options that you can select with the commands in the View menu. For example, you can change the view to display files and directories on two disk drives.

To display the files and directories on your hard disk drive and your floppy disk drive, perform the steps in one or both of the following two procedures.

Changing the View with the Mouse

① Click the appropriate drive icon to select the hard disk drive.

② Click the View menu.

③ Click the Dual File Lists command.

The main part of the Shell display is now split into an upper and lower section. Both sections display directories and files for your hard disk drive (see Figure 6.2).

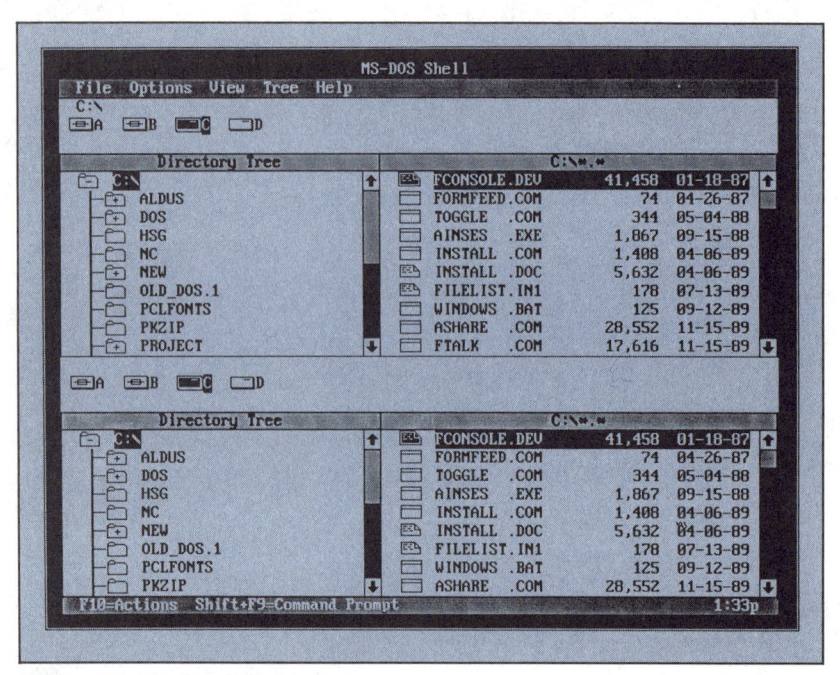

Figure 6.2: The Dual File Lists view

To display directories for your floppy disk drive, follow these steps:

① Insert a floppy diskette that contains information into your floppy disk drive.

② Click the appropriate drive icon in the lower display area to select the floppy diskette drive.

The lower display area now shows the directories and files from your floppy disk drive.

To return to the original Shell view, select the Program/Files List command from the View menu.

Changing the View with the Keyboard

① Press Alt to select the menu bar.

② Press V to open the View menu.

③ Press D to select the Dual File Lists command.

The main part of the Shell is now split into an upper and lower section. Both sections display directories and files for your hard disk drive (see Figure 6.2).

To display directories for your floppy disk drive, follow these steps:

① Insert a floppy diskette that contains information into your floppy disk drive.

② Press Tab until one of the drive icons in the lower section is highlighted.

③ Press the right arrow key (→) or left arrow key (←) until the appropriate drive icon for your floppy disk drive is highlighted.

④ Press ↵.

The lower display area now shows the directories and files from your floppy disk drive.

To return to the original Shell view, select the Program/Files List command from the View menu.

Working with the Directory Tree

When you select a directory in the directory tree, its files are displayed in the file area to the right. The current directory tree shows the root directory and all first-level directories on your hard disk drive. You can change this display to show only the root directory or to show subdirectories for one or more directory.

Selecting a Directory

To select the DOS directory with the mouse, click the DOS directory icon. The file area now displays all the files in the DOS directory.

To select the DOS directory with the keyboard, follow these steps:

1. Press Tab until the directory tree area is selected.
2. Press the ↑ or ↓ until the DOS directory icon is highlighted.

The file list area now displays all the files in the DOS directory.

Changing the Directory Tree Display

Some directory icons may contain a plus sign (+). This indicates that that directory contains at least one subdirectory, and you can expand the directory tree to display the branches for the subdirectories. The root directory icon contains a minus sign (−), which indicates that you can collapse the display so that only the root directory is displayed.

To collapse the display using the mouse, click the minus sign (−) on the root directory icon. The directory tree now displays only the root directory. The directory icon contains a plus sign (+).

To collapse the display using the keyboard, follow these steps:

1. Press Tab to select the directory tree area.
2. Press ↑ or ↓ to select the root directory icon.
3. Press the minus sign (−) key.

The directory tree now displays only the root directory. The directory icon contains a plus sign (+).

To expand the display using the mouse, click the plus sign (+) on the root directory icon. The directory tree now displays the root directory and the first-level directory branch.

To expand the display using the keyboard, follow these steps:

1. Make sure that the root directory icon is still selected or press Tab to select it.
2. Press the plus sign (+) key. If you do not have a numeric keyboard, you must hold down the Shift key and press the plus sign key.

The directory tree now displays the root directory and the first-level directory branch. You can also use the Tree menu commands to modify the directory tree display.

To collapse the first-level directory branch, perform the steps in one or both of the following two procedures.

Using the Mouse

1. Click the Tree menu.
2. Click the Collapse Branch command.

The directory tree now displays only the root directory. The directory icon contains a plus sign (+).

Using the Keyboard

1. Press Alt to select the menu bar.
2. Press T to display the Tree menu.
3. Press C to select the Collapse Branch command.

The directory tree now displays only the root directory. The directory icon contains a plus sign (+).

To expand the branch of the root directory, peform the steps in one or both of the following two procedures.

Using the Mouse

① Click the Tree menu.

② Click the Expand One Level command.

The directory tree now displays the root directory and the branch with the first level directories.

Using the Keyboard

① Press Alt to select the menu bar.

② Press T to display the Tree menu.

③ Press X to select the Expand One Level command.

The directory tree now displays the root directory and the branch with the first level directories.

Working with the File Area

The file area lists the files in the directory that is selected in the corresponding directory tree. You can change the order of the list, move files between directories, and run executable files.

Sorting Files

The current file area probably displays files in alphabetical order according to file names. You can change this order by selecting one of the file display options available in the Options menu.

To sort the files by date, perform the steps in one or both of the following two procedures.

Using the Mouse to Sort Files

① Click the Options menu.

② Click the File Display Options command.

The Display Options dialog box appears. It contains options for controlling the file display. At the right of the box is a list of selections for sorting files. Each selection has a button at its left.

③ Click the Date button.

④ Click OK to close the dialog box.

The file list display is now sorted by date.

Using the Keyboard to Sort Files

① Press Alt to select the menu bar.

② Press O to open the Options menu.

③ Press F to select the File Display Options command.

The Display Options dialog box appears, containing options for setting the file display. At the right of the box is a list of selections for sorting files. Each selection has a button at its left. The Name option is currently selected.

④ Press Tab until the Sort by list is selected.

⑤ Press ↓ to select the Date button.

⑥ Press ⏎ to close the dialog box.

The file list display is now sorted by date.

Other Sorting Options

Besides the Sort by options, the Display Options dialog box also contains options for displaying hidden and system files and for displaying files in descending order. The Descending order option works with all of the choices in the Sort by list. To select the option using the mouse, click in the brackets preceding the option. To select this option using the keyboard, follow these steps:

① Press Tab until the cursor is under the brackets for the Descending order option.

② Press the spacebar.

③ An X appears within the brackets.

④ Press ↵ to close the dialog box.

Creating a File

For the next series of exercises, you need to create a test file in the root directory. If you already know a procedure for creating a file, follow that procedure and name the file TEST.FIL. If you don't know how to create a file, follow these steps:

① Using either the mouse or the keyboard, select Command Prompt in the Main Group to get the DOS command line.

② At the DOS prompt, type

COPY CON TEST.FIL

and press ↵.

③ Type

This is a test file.

④ Hold down Ctrl and press Z. ^Z appears at the end of your text line.

⑤ Press ↵.

⑥ At the DOS prompt, type

exit

to return to the DOS Shell.

To verify that the file TEST.FIL has been created, select the root directory. In the file area, press ↑ or ↓ or click the mouse on the scroll bar's down arrow to scroll through the list until TEST.FIL is displayed.

Now that you have a file to work with, you can practice using some of the Shell's file manipulation options. You can use the Shell to copy and move files between directories, rename a file, or delete one from a directory.

NOTE: In this next series of exercises, we use the DOS directory as the second directory. If you have additional directories on your hard disk drive, use one of them instead of the DOS directory. If you use the DOS directory, you should be careful not to alter or delete any files other than your test file.

Selecting Files

In the next few exercises, you will need to select a file in the file area. To select a file with the mouse, click that file. To select it with the keyboard, press ↑ or ↓ until the file is highlighted.

You can also select and work with groups of files. If you want to select more than one file, you can choose files that are in a sequence in the file list or you can choose files that are scattered throughout the list.

To select a group of files in sequence, perform the steps in one or both of the following two procedures.

Using the Mouse

① Click the first file that you want included in the group.

② Hold down the Shift key and click the last file that you want included.

Using the Keyboard

① Press ↑ or ↓ to select the first file that you want included in the group.

② Hold down the Shift key and press ↑ or ↓ to select all the files that you want included.

To select a group of files not in sequence, perform the steps in one or both of the following two procedures.

Using the Mouse

① Press and hold the Ctrl key down.

② Click each file that you want included in the group.

Using the Keyboard

① Hold down the Shift key and press the F8 function key. The status bar displays the message **Add.**

② Press ↑ or ↓ to move to the first file that you want included.

③ Press the spacebar to select that file.

④ Repeat steps 2 and 3 for each file that you want included.

⑤ Hold down the Shift key and press F8 again to complete the selection.

Copying a File to Another Directory

To copy TEST.FIL from the root directory to the DOS directory, perform the steps in one or both of the following two procedures.

Using the Mouse to Copy a File

① Select the root directory icon in the directory tree.

② Position the mouse pointer over TEST.FIL in the file area. Don't click yet.

③ Hold down the Ctrl key, then press and hold the mouse button.

④ Drag TEST.FIL to the DOS directory icon in the directory tree.

⑤ Release the mouse button.

The Confirm Mouse Operation dialog box appears and asks if you want to copy the selected file.

⑥ Click Yes to confirm the operation and close the dialog box.

To verify that TEST.FIL has been copied, select the DOS directory in the directory tree and scroll through the file list until TEST.FIL appears in the window.

Using the Keyboard to Copy a File

① Select the root directory icon in the directory tree.

② Make the file area active and select TEST.FIL.

③ Select the Copy command from the File menu.

The Copy File dialog box appears. The From: text box displays the file that you are copying. The To: text box displays the current path of the file.

④ Type **C:\DOS** in the To: text box to change the destination directory.

⑤ Press ← to close the dialog box.

To verify that TEST.FIL has been copied, select the DOS directory in the directory tree and scroll through the file list until TEST.FIL appears in the window.

Renaming a File

To rename TEST.FIL, follow these steps:

① Select TEST.FIL from the file list.

② Select the Rename command in the File menu.

The Rename File dialog box appears. It identifies the file's current name as TEST.FIL. The New name text box is empty.

③ Type **TEST.DOC** in the New name text box to rename the file.

④ Click OK or press ← to close the dialog box.

To verify that the file is renamed, scroll through the file list until TEST.DOC is displayed.

Moving a File

Moving a file differs from copying a file. When you copy a file, the file stays in the original directory and is duplicated in the new directory. When you move a file, it is removed from the original directory and transferred to the new directory.

To move TEST.DOC from the DOS directory to the root directory, follow the steps in one or both of the following two procedures.

Using the Mouse

1. Select the DOS directory in the directory tree.
2. Position the mouse pointer over TEST.DOC in the file area.
3. Hold down the mouse button and drag TEST.DOC to the root directory icon in the directory tree.
4. Release the mouse button.

   The Confirm Mouse Operation dialog box appears and asks if you want to move the selected file.
5. Click Yes to confirm the operation and close the dialog box.

To verify that the file has been moved, select the DOS directory in the directory tree, then scroll through the file list until TEST.DOC is displayed.

Using the Keyboard

1. Select TEST.DOC from the file list.
2. Select the Move command from the File menu.

   The Move File dialog box appears. The From: text box identifies the file that you are moving. The To: text box displays the current path of the file.

③ Type **C:** into the To: text box to change the destination directory.

④ Press ⏎ to close the dialog box.

To verify that the file has been moved, select the DOS directory in the directory tree, then scroll through the file list until TEST.DOC is displayed.

Deleting a File

To delete TEST.DOC from the root directory, follow these steps:

① Select TEST.DOC from the file list.

② Select the Delete command from the File menu.

The Delete File dialog box appears. The Delete text box displays the name of the selected file.

③ Click OK or press ⏎ to close the dialog box.

The Delete File Confirmation dialog box appears and asks if you want to delete the selected file.

④ Click Yes or press ⏎ to confirm the command.

Running Executable Files

You can run any executable files from the file area. The common extensions for executable files are .EXE, .COM, and .BAT. To run an executable file, simply double-click it.

The DOS CHKDSK command checks a disk's size and displays information about the current use of disk space.

To run CHKDSK from the file list, follow these steps:

① Select the file list area.

② Double-click CHKDSK.EXE.

When CHKDSK is finished, the screen displays a report about your disk and prompts you to press any key to continue.

③ Press any key to return to the DOS Shell.

Working with the Program Area

The program area displays available program items and program groups. Each group is a collection of program items; by selecting a program item, you can run its associated file.

The icons for program groups and program items are similar; the icon for a program group is filled with small boxes, while the program item icon is empty.

Your program area contains the Main group and the Disk Utilities Group. These groups give you quick and easy access to some helpful DOS commands. As you become more familiar with the Shell, you can add other program items and groups. If you want to modify the program area, refer to your DOS documentation for instructions. In this chapter, we provide basic instructions for using the groups already in the program area.

If the Main group is not open, use the mouse or the keyboard to open it. It contains three program items and the Disk Utilities group. MS-DOS\QBASIC Editor is a text editing program, and MS-DOS QBASIC provides a simple environment for programming in the BASIC language. The third item, Command Prompt, provides a quick means of getting to a DOS prompt.

The Disk Utilities Group contains six DOS utilities. Disk Copy lets you copy information from one floppy disk to another. Backup Fixed Disk lets you backup all or selected files and directories from your hard disk. Restore Fixed Disk lets you restore these files. Quick Format lets you format previously formatted disks that you know are in good condition. Undelete lets you restore files that have been previously deleted with the DEL command.

Format lets you format floppy disks from the DOS Shell. To format a floppy, follow these steps:

① Select Format from the Program area.

The Format dialog box appears. The Parameters text box displays the drive letter for your floppy disk drive. If it is not the correct drive, press the backspace arrow (←) to erase the drive and type in the appropriate drive letter, followed by a colon (:).

② Click OK or press ← to close the dialog box.

The system exits the DOS Shell. The screen display instructs you to insert a floppy disk into the appropriate drive and to press ←.

③ Insert an unformatted disk into the floppy drive and press ←.

When the disk is formatted, the display asks for a volume label.

④ Don't enter a label for this disk. Press ← to continue.

The display asks if you want to format another disk.

⑤ Type **N** and press ←.

The display instructs you to press any key to continue.

⑥ Press any key to return to the DOS Shell.

Using the Task Swapper

The DOS Shell allows you to keep more than one program in memory and switch back and forth between them. This feature can be helpful if you use certain programs frequently; you can collect the programs in the Active Task List and use that area to switch between them.

If the Active Task List window isn't already visible, select the Enable Task Swapper command from the Options menu. The Active Task List is displayed in the lower right corner of the Shell and is currently empty (see Figure 6.3). To add a program to the Active Task List, you start the program and then hold down the Alt key and press Tab to return to the Shell.

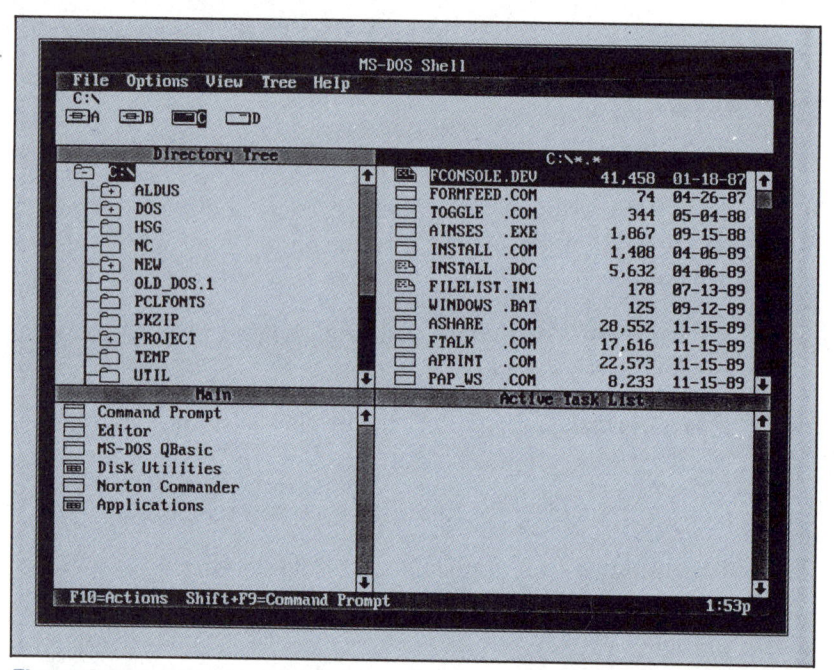

Figure 6.3: The Task List area

To add MS-DOS Command Prompt and Format to the Task List, follow these steps:

① Activate Command Prompt from the Main area.

② At the DOS prompt, hold down the Alt key and press Tab to return to the Shell.

③ Activate Format from the Disk Utilities Group.

④ The Format dialog box appears. Click OK or press ↵.

The screen prompts you to insert a disk in the floppy drive.

⑤ Instead of inserting a disk, hold down the Alt key and press Tab to return to the Shell.

MS-DOS Command Prompt and Format are displayed in the Active Task List.

To switch between MS-DOS Command Prompt and Format, follow these steps:

① Activate MS-DOS Command Prompt by selecting it from the Task List.

② At the DOS prompt, type

   exit

   to return to the Shell.

③ Activate Format by selecting it from the Task List.

④ Follow the screen instructions to format a floppy diskette and return to the Shell.

Review

The DOS Shell

- Is a graphical interface for your computer's disk operating system.
- Lets you organize files and directories on your hard and floppy disk drives.
- Lets you run multiple programs simultaneously and switch back and forth between them.
- Provides easy access to your most frequently used files.

Chapter 7

Windows 3.0 Work Session

Featuring

Arranging the windows display on your desktop

Switching back and forth between your documents

Running multiple applications simultaneously

You can choose from a large variety of Windows programs to run on your PC. Word-processing applications, databases, and games are just some of the types available. Whether you decide to install one application or many, the Windows graphical environment gives you greater file-management control and lets you arrange applications and documents on the desktop to meet your viewing needs.

Windows 3.0 enables your computer to run a number of programs at the same time, and allows you to switch back and forth between these program at your convenience. This can be especially helpful if a program is working on a task that will take awhile to complete, such as performing many calculations or printing complex graphics. Rather than simply waiting for this program to complete its work, you can switch to another program and keep working. The first program will continue to operate in the background.

Some programs are specially designed to work with Windows 3.0—such as Word for Windows, Excel, and ToolBook. You cannot use these programs unless your computer is running Windows. However, Windows also works with programs that were not designed for it. You might not be able to display these programs within Windows, depending on the type of computer that you have and the *mode* in which you are running Windows. If a program cannot be displayed within Windows, it will run in *full-screen* mode. This means that the program will fill the entire screen.

This chapter is not intended to give you a comprehensive understanding of Windows; instead, it provides a general introduction. We take you through a series of exercises that use the basic features you need to get started in Windows.

We assume that you have already installed Windows 3.0 on your hard disk. You should refer to the Windows documentation for installation instructions.

Running Windows on a 386 Computer

A 386 computer has a microprocessor that is better than earlier processors at performing complex memory operations. Because many Windows operations involve juggling memory, Windows, like other programs, runs better on a 386. A major advantage is that you can run programs that were not designed for Windows in a window. If you are using a computer with a processor earlier than the 386, Windows will only run these programs in full-screen mode, which makes it more cumbersome for you to switch between programs.

Loading Windows

The first step is to start Windows. If you are using the DOS command line, make the Windows directory your current directory. At the command prompt, type

WIN

and press ⏎. If you are using the DOS shell, select the Windows directory, then the Win.com icon to start the Windows program.

The Program Manager Window

The very first time that you start Windows, the Program Manager window opens (see Figure 7.1). After this first time, the opening screen will vary, depending on whether or not you saved the previous session. The Program Manager is a Windows application that lets you open and organize applications.

If the Program Manager isn't open, you can open it with your mouse (if you have one) or with the keyboard. To open the window with the mouse, place the mouse pointer on the Program Manager icon and double-click the mouse. To open it with the keyboard, hold down the Alt key and press the spacebar to open the Control menu, and then press R to select the Restore command.

Most of the elements in the Program Manager window are common to all Windows programs. The following list identifies these elements and gives a brief explanation of their functions. We provide

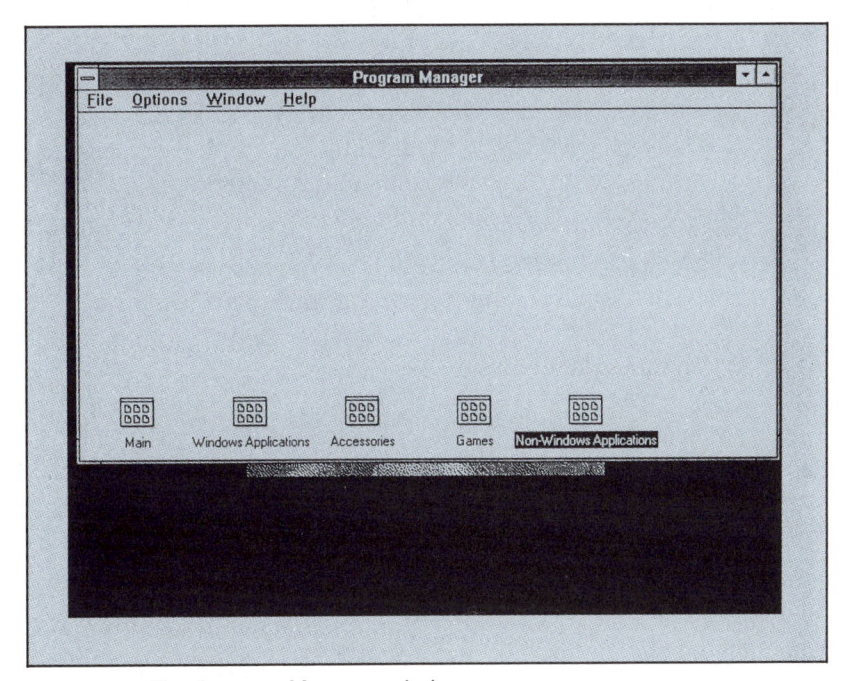

Figure 7.1: The Program Manager window

more detailed instructions about each feature as you use it in the chapter exercises.

- The Control menu allows you to control the size and movement of windows and to transfer information between files. To see the Control menu, click the Control menu box—the small rectangle in the window's upper-left corner.
- The Title bar identifies the window.
- The Minimize and Maximize buttons let you shrink the open window to an icon or enlarge the window to fill the desktop. The Minimize and Maximize buttons are the arrows located in the window's upper-right corner.
- The Menu bar displays the menus that contain the commands for the application or document. The Program Manager menu bar contains the File, Options, Window, and Help menus.
- The Workspace is the large area in the center of the window. The Program Manager's workspace contains group icons and/or windows. A group is a set of related applications and documents. Your Program Manager workspace displays the Accessories, Games, and Main group icons and, depending on your installation process, might also display the Windows and Non-Windows Application Group Icons.
- The Window borders and corners let you alter the size and shape of a window. You can use the borders to change the length or height of one side of a window, and you can use the corners to change two sides simultaneously.

Opening an Application Window

For the moment, you are finished with the Program Manager; you know the names and basic functions of its main elements and are ready to move on. The next section takes you quickly through the steps for opening another kind of window, an application window. You will open Write, which is the word-processing program that is provided by Windows in the Accessories group.

The Write icon is contained in the Accessories group window. If the window is currently closed and displayed as the Accessories group icon, you need to open the group window before you can start Write.

Using the Mouse to Open Write

The easiest way to open a second window from the Program Manager is to use a mouse. If you have a mouse, you will see the mouse pointer on your screen (see Figure 7.2). When you move the mouse around on a flat surface, the pointer moves.

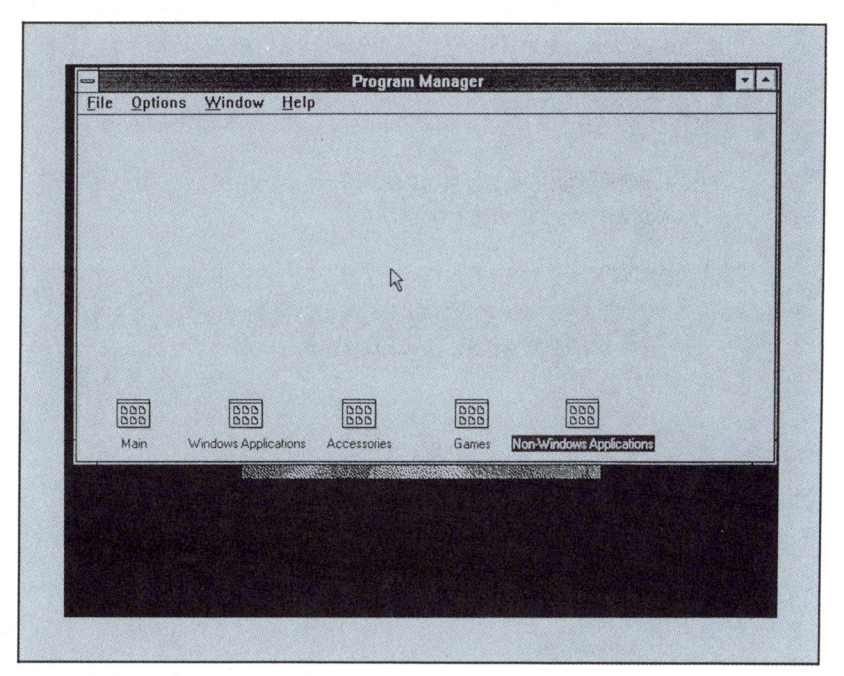

Figure 7.2: The mouse pointer

① Open the Accessories window by moving the pointer to the Accessories group icon and double-clicking the mouse button.

The Accessories window appears. It contains icons for the applications in the group.

② Click the Write icon. The Write application window opens (see Figure 7.3).

Using the Keyboard

① When using the keyboard, open group windows by using the commands in the Window menu. Open the Window menu by pressing the Alt key then pressing W.

The bottom section of the Window menu contains a numbered list of the groups available in the Program Manager. The order of the list will vary depending on the groups' arrangement in the Program Manager window.

② To open the Accessories window, press the appropriate number.

The Accessories window appears. It contains the icons for the applications in the group.

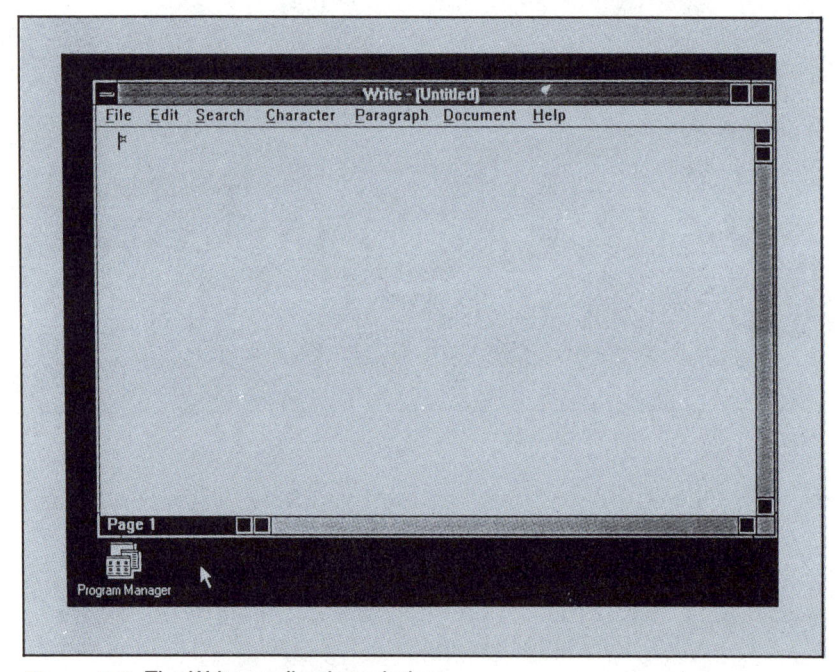

Figure 7.3: The Write application window

③ The Write icon name might be highlighted to indicate that it is selected. If it is not selected, use the direction keys to move through the Accessories icons until the icon is selected.

④ To start the Write application, press ↵.

The Write Application Window opens (see Figure 7.3).

Elements of an Application Window

An application window might be very similar to the Program Manager window. As you can see, all of the elements in the Program Manager window are present in the Write window. However, some of the elements have slightly different functions in this window. The following list identifies these differences.

- In an application window, the title bar contains the name of the application and of the associated document that is open. As you can see in the figure, the title bar in the Write application window identifies both Write and an "untitled" document. **Note:** Some applications, such as Write, automatically open a new document when you start them. Others require additional commands to open a document.

- In an application window, the menu bar contains menus for the open application and document.

- Application windows also contain scroll bars, which are not usually present in the Program Manager window. The scroll bars (and the boxes and arrows on the scroll bars) let you move through a window to view different parts of its contents.

Working with Menus

Now that you've identified the basic features of a window, you need to know how to use the mouse and the keyboard to work with menus.

You can use the mouse and the keyboard independently or in combination to execute menu commands within Windows. Wherever applicable in this chapter, we give you instructions for using each tool. As you become more familiar with Windows, you will make your own decisions about using the mouse or the keyboard in a given situation.

To get Help information about Write commands, perform the steps in one or both of the following two procedures.

Using the Mouse

① Position the mouse pointer on the Help menu in the Write window.

② Click the mouse and release the button.

The Help menu commands are displayed. Notice that the first command is selected.

③ Move the pointer to Commands and click.

A window opens, displaying instructions for getting information about Write commands.

④ Click the File menu in the Help window.

⑤ Click the Exit command to close the Help window.

Using the Keyboard

① Press the Alt key and then press H to open the Help menu in the Write window.

The Help menu commands are displayed. Notice that the first command is selected.

② Press C to select Commands.

A window opens, displaying instructions for getting information about Write commands.

③ Press the Alt key and then press F to open the File menu in the Help window.

④ Press ⏎ to close the Help window.

*W*orking with a Single Window

Now that you're more familiar with Windows, you can start using what you've learned. In the next series of exercises, you will type a letter in Write and apply some of the features that we've discussed in the previous sections.

The selection cursor is already positioned at the top of the window, ready for you to start typing.

① Type the following letter:

Dear Mr. Leone:

We have received the party supply request for your son Marco's first birthday. Per your letter, we will deliver the following items:

1 layer cake

2 gallons ice cream

5 cartons diapers

1 Twister for Toddlers

1 mariachi band with Elvis impersonator

Our bill

We appreciate this opportunity to serve you.

Sincerely,

Ana Gabriel
Vice President
The Gift Is in the Giving Catering Company

Saving a Document

It is always a good idea to save documents as you write in order to ensure that no material is lost. Saving a document does not close the window.

To save your letter, perform the steps in one or both of the following two procedures.

Using the Mouse

① Click the File menu.

② Move the pointer to the Save command and click.

A dialog box appears, asking you to name the document that you want to save.

③ To name the document, type the following into the Filename box:

LEONE

.WRI is the filename extension for a Write file. The extension is automatically appended to any file created in Write.

④ Click the OK button.

Using the Keyboard

① Open the File menu by pressing the Alt key and then pressing F.

② Press S to select the Save command.

A dialog box appears, asking you to name the document.

③ To name the document, type the following into the Filename box:

LEONE

.WRI is the filename extension for a Write file. The extension is automatically appended to any file created in Write.

④ Press ↵.

Changing the Size of a Window

The letter is too large to fit within the Write window. Windows provides several ways in which you can change the view of a window.

You can adjust the size of the window to see more of the document. By using the mouse, keyboard, and menus, you can increase the height and/or the width of the window.

To widen the window, perform the steps in one or both of the following procedures.

Dragging with the Mouse

① Position the mouse pointer on the window's left border. The mouse pointer icon changes to a double arrow pointing left and right.

② Hold the mouse button down and drag the border slightly to the left. You can see the outline of the border move as you drag it.

③ Release the mouse button.

Dragging with the Keyboard

① Open the Control menu by holding down the Alt key and pressing the spacebar.

② Press S to select the Size command. The mouse pointer icon changes to a cross.

③ Press the left direction key (←) to move the border slightly to the left. The mouse pointer changes to a double arrow pointing left and right. You can see the outline of the border move as you press ←.

④ Press ↵.

At this point, the window is not large enough to display the entire letter. Rather than continue to drag the borders, however, it would be easier for you to open the window to its largest size. This is called maximizing.

To maximize the window, perform the steps in one or both of the following two procedures.

Maximizing with the Mouse

① Click the maximize button. The window for LEONE.WRI now fills the entire desktop.

Maximizing with the Keyboard

① Open the Control menu by holding down the Alt key and pressing the spacebar.

② Press X to select the Maximize command.

You now see a much greater part of the letter than was visible in the original window. Even at this size, however, part of the letter is still out of view. To look at the remainder of the letter, you will need to scroll through it.

Scrolling through a Window

You can view different parts of a document by scrolling through its window at varying increments. If you have a mouse, you use the scroll bars at the side and the bottom of the window. If you are using your keyboard, you will type specific keys to view the window. Practice scrolling through the document LEONE.WRI.

Using the Mouse

For this exercise, scroll through the length of the letter by using the scroll bar at the side of the window. This will allow you to scroll up and down through the letter. The bottom scroll bar lets you scroll sideways through a document.

① Click the ↓ on the scroll bar. The letter scrolls up one line.

② Keep the mouse pointer positioned over the ↓ and hold the mouse button down. The letter now scrolls up continuously so that you can view the display as it moves through the window. To stop the scrolling movement, release the mouse button.

③ Click the scroll bar at any point above the scroll box. The letter scrolls down one full window.

④ Position the mouse pointer on the scroll box, hold down the mouse button and drag the box to the end of the scroll bar. The letter scrolls to the end of the document.

By dragging the scroll box, you can scroll through a document to the approximate section of your choice.

Using the Keyboard

① Press the down direction key (↓) until the cursor is in the last line of the window.

② Press the ↓ key once. The selection cursor scrolls down one line.

Hold down the ↓ key. The selection cursor scrolls continuously down so that you can view the display as it moves through the window.

③ Press the Page Down key once. The letter scrolls up one full window.

④ Hold the Ctrl key down and press End. The letter scrolls to the end of the document.

To move back to the beginning of the document, hold the Ctrl key down and press Home.

Working with Two or More Windows

With Windows, you are not limited to working in one document or file at a time. In this series of exercises, you will use the features that you've learned to work within more than one file.

Now that you've written the letter to Mr. Leone, you need to find his address and insert it at the top of the letter. Windows includes another application in its Accessories group that can help you with this task. Cardfile is organized like the address file on your desk; it contains a series of blank "cards" on which you can enter the addresses of your friends, co-workers, and customers.

To open Cardfile, you must return to the Program Manager window. At this point, you cannot see the Program Manager icon because the Write window covers the entire desktop. Instead of using borders to resize the window, however, you can use another method, the Windows Restore feature.

Restoring with the Mouse

When you maximized the Write window, the Maximize button was replaced with the Restore button. The Restore button is the double arrow in the box next to the Minimize button (see Figure 7.4).

To return the Write window to its previous size, click the Restore button. You can now see the Program Manager icon at the bottom of

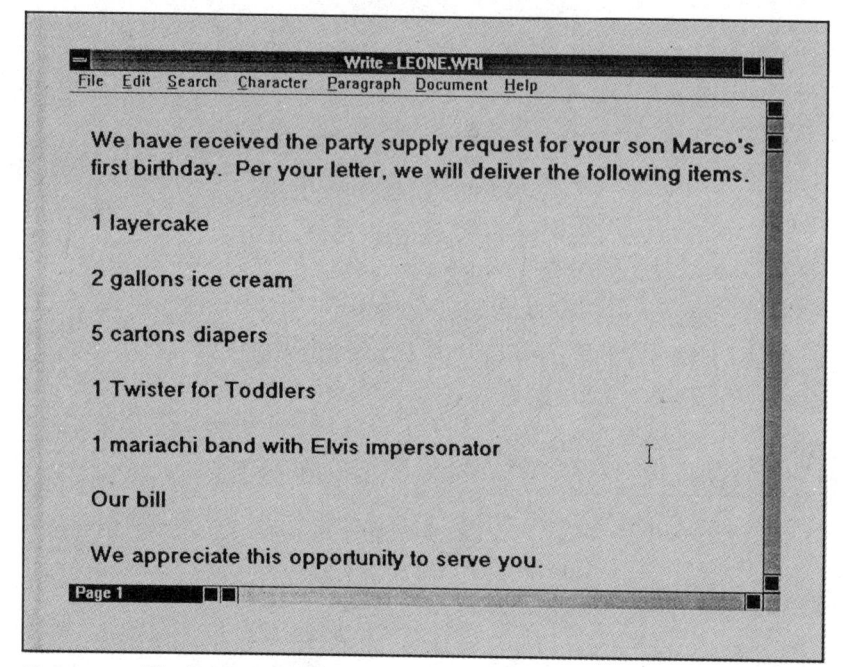

Figure 7.4: The Restore button

the desktop or, if the Minimize on Use command is not enabled, the Program Manager window behind the Write window.

Restoring with the Keyboard

① Open the Control menu.

② Press R to select the Restore command and to return the Write window to its previous size.

You can now see the Program Manager icon at the bottom of the desktop or, if the Minimize on Use command is not enabled, the Program Manager window behind the Write window.

Starting in Cardfile

The Cardfile application is in the Accessories group. To open the Accessories group, you must first reopen the Program Manager window or bring it to the foreground if it is already open.

To open a Cardfile window, perform the steps in one or both of the two following procedures.

Using the Mouse

① If the Program Manager is an icon, double-click the icon. If the Program Manager is a Window, click the window.

② Click the Accessories group icon to open the Accessories window.

③ To start Cardfile, double-click the Cardfile icon.

Using the Keyboard

If the Program Manager is an icon, follow the steps in the list. If the Program Manager is a window, press the Alt key, then press Esc, and begin with step 4.

① Hold down the Alt key and press Esc. The Program Manager icon is highlighted.

② To open the Program Manager window, hold down the Alt key and press the spacebar. The Control menu is displayed.

③ Press R to restore the icon to a window.

④ Use the direction keys to highlight the Accessories icon, and then press ⏎.

⑤ Use the direction keys to highlight the Cardfile icon, and then press ⏎.

Working in Cardfile

The Cardfile window is now open on the desktop. Like Write, Cardfile automatically opens a new document file when it is started. The first card is displayed in the window. The selection cursor is positioned at the top of the card, ready for you to type.

① Type the following information into the card. Press ⏎ after each line.

   Vicente Leone
   212 Tipu St.
   Mountain View, CA 94303

Use the mouse or the keyboard to choose the Save command from the File menu. A dialog box opens, asking you to name the document. Type **LEONE**, then click OK or press ⏎. A .CRD extension is appended to the file name for a Cardfile document; the extension is automatically appended to any file created in Cardfile.

You now have the information that you need. In a few minutes, you will transfer the address from the card file to the letter. With Windows, you can do this easily by displaying the Cardfile and Write windows simultaneously. Before you transfer, however, let's see how you can arrange the windows to facilitate your work.

Arranging Windows on the Desktop

At this point, you should be able to see parts of the three open windows, although the Cardfile and Program Manager windows cover most of the Write window. To help you quickly identify the active window, its menu bar and borders are of a different intensity (or color, if you have a color monitor) than those of the inactive windows. The Cardfile window is currently the active window.

Windows offers several ways for you to arrange windows on your desktop. You can reduce the size of windows, you can move them around, and you can switch back and forth between them, even if they are not all immediately visible. You should practice arranging windows on your desktop.

Moving Windows with the Mouse

① Position the mouse pointer on the Cardfile title bar. Hold the mouse button down and drag the window to the right. You can see the outline of the window move as you drag it.

② To place the window in its new position, release the mouse button.

Moving Windows with the Keyboard

① Open the Control menu.

② Press M to select the Move command.

The mouse pointer icon changes to a cross. You use the direction keys to move the window around on the desktop.

③ To move the window down, press the ↓ key. You can see the outline of the window move as you press the key.

④ To place the window in its new position, press ⏎.

Windows provides two automatic features to simplify your display choices—the Cascade and Tile options. You can access both of these features with the Switch To command.

Automatically Arranging Windows with the Mouse

To arrange windows with the Cascade feature, follow these

steps:

① Open the Control menu.

② Select the Switch To command.

The Task List dialog box opens, displaying several buttons that you can select, including the Cascade button.

③ Click the Cascade button.

The dialog box closes, and the two open windows are arranged in a diagonally cascading pattern over the desktop.

Automatically Arranging Windows with the Keyboard

To arrange windows with the Tile feature, follow these steps:

① Hold down the Alt key and press the Spacebar to open the Control menu.

② Press W to select the Switch To command.

The Task List dialog box opens, displaying several buttons that you can select, including the Tile button. You can tell which button is currently selected because it is surrounded by a heavier border than the others.

③ Press Tab until the Tile button is selected.

④ Press ←⎯.

The dialog box closes.

The open windows are now arranged side-by-side across the desktop. Now that you have the Write and Cardfile windows arranged on your desktop, you can transfer information between them. Windows lets you switch back and forth between windows with ease.

Transferring Information between Windows

First, you need to copy the necessary information from Cardfile. If the Cardfile window is not the active window, click the Cardfile window or hold down the Alt key and press Esc until it is active.

To copy the Leone address, perform the steps in one or both of the following two procedures.

Copying Text with the Mouse

① To place the cursor at the beginning of the text, position the mouse pointer before the *V* in Vicente and click the mouse.

② Hold the mouse button down, drag the pointer downward until the entire address is highlighted, and then release the button.

③ Select the Copy command from the Edit menu.

Copying Text with the Keyboard

① Use the direction keys to position the selection cursor in front of the *V* in Vicente.

② Hold the Shift key down and press the right direction arrow (→) until the entire address is highlighted.

③ Select the Copy command from the Edit menu.

Changing the Active Window

Now that you have copied the address, you need to paste it into the letter in Write. To do this you must activate the Write window. Click the Write window or press the Alt key and press Esc until the Write window is active.

Changing the Window with Switch To

In this exercise, you have only a few windows open and you can see part of each one. There might be times during your own work sessions when you have multiple windows open or when there is no visible part of a window to click. In these cases, you can use the Switch To command.

① Use the mouse or the keyboard to open the Control menu.

② Select the Switch To command.

The Task List dialog box opens. Besides the buttons you used earlier, the dialog box also displays a list of active windows. The list currently contains LEONE.WRI, LEONE.CRD, and Program Manager.

③ To select LEONE.WRI, double-click the entry or highlight it with the ↓ key and press ⏎.

The Write window is now the active window and is at the front of the desktop. You can paste the address from Cardfile into the letter.

To paste the address into the letter, perform the steps in one or both of the following two procedures.

Pasting Text with the Mouse

① Position the mouse pointer before the *D* in Dear and click the mouse.

② Press ⏎ twice to add space at the beginning of the letter.

③ Open the Edit menu and select Paste.

Pasting Text with the Keyboard

① Use the direction keys to position the selection cursor in front of the *D* in Dear.

② To add space at the beginning of the letter, press ⏎ twice.

③ To select the Paste command, open the Edit menu and press P.

Mr. Leone's address is now incorporated into the letter. You can use the mouse or the keyboard to save the revised document.

Review

Windows:

- Is a helpful file-management program.
- Provides several helpful accessory applications for you to use.
- Lets you arrange the window display on your desktop.
- Makes it easy for you to switch back and forth between open documents.
- Allows you to run multiple applications simultaneously.

Part IV

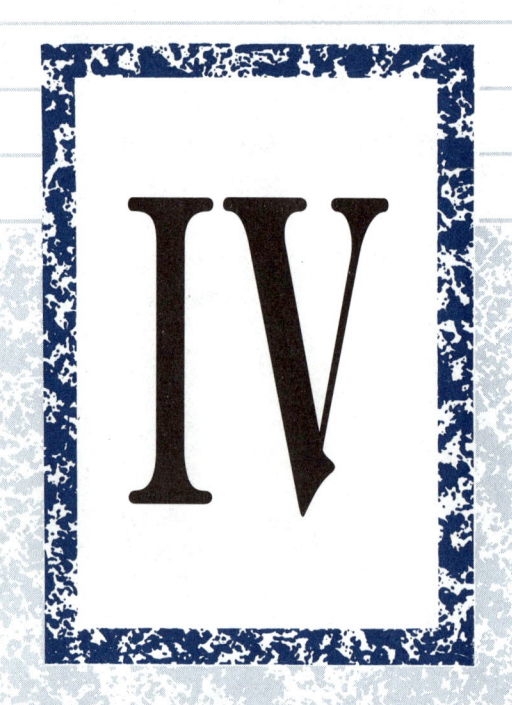

Using Applications

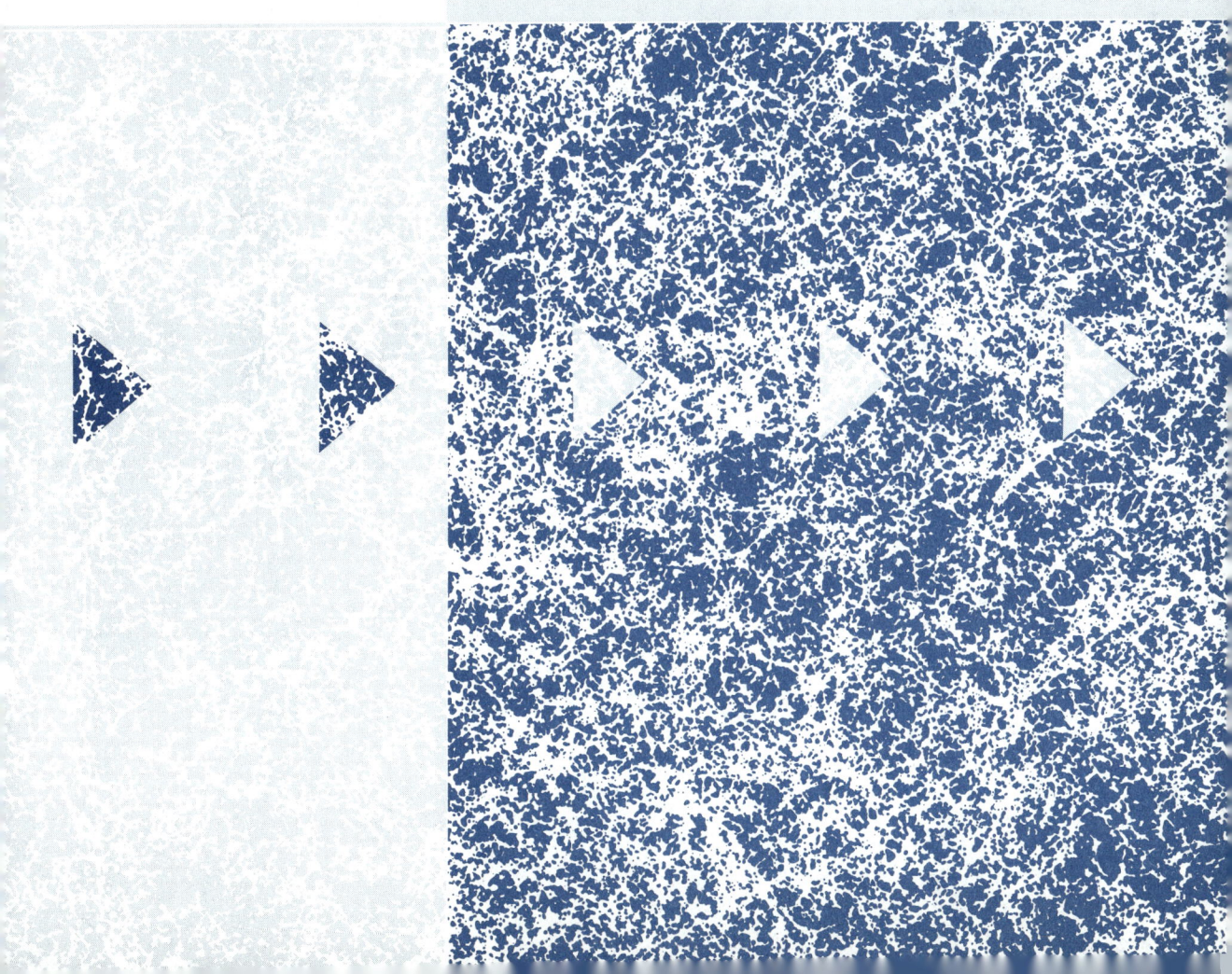

Chapter 8

Computer Applications: Tools for Your PC

*F*eaturing

Installing, backing up, and loading an application

Entering, saving, retrieving, revising, and printing information

So I know about diskettes and files and DOS commands and menus and function keys, you are saying. *What happens now?* Well, this is the moment you've been waiting for! We are going to talk about application programs, the tools that put your computer to work for you.

Application programs take personal computers out of the domain of the technical expert and turn them into useful and productive tools for everyone. The majority of people use their PCs with application programs selected to meet their particular needs. So this chapter introduces you to applications. You will see that all our rules about disks and files are for good reason. Any application you use relies on disks to store your information and file names to identify the information you want to work with. Before you purchase an application, be sure you can use it with your PC. Some applications require additional memory or a special monitor or adapter.

Installing an Application

The process of copying an application program from the diskette on which it is distributed to your hard disk is called *installing* the application. The application program may consist of one or more files, and the diskette on which it is distributed may contain different versions of files for different types of PCs. Often, you must create a special directory on the hard disk for the application. For these reasons, it does not make sense to install an application by simply copying all of the files from the distribution diskette to your hard disk.

Follow the software manufacturer's instructions for installing an application program. Sometimes applications come with programs that copy the appropriate files for you. All you do is answer questions that the program asks about your system.

In Chapter 9 we will introduce you to two applications, a word processor and a financial spreadsheet. We use the two currently most popular programs, WordPerfect and Lotus 1-2-3. If you have these two programs, install them on your PC now. If you do not, install the word processing and spreadsheet programs you have; you may be able to follow many of our instructions anyway.

Making a Backup Copy

As we said in Chapter 4, it is a good practice to make a backup of your important diskettes. This is just as true for application program diskettes as it is for DOS and your information files. Once you have installed an application, you should make a copy of it. Store the duplicate and the original diskette in a safe place. If anything ever happens to the installed version, you can always make another copy from the original or the duplicate.

① Turn on your PC, if it is not on already.

② To begin copying the diskette, insert the application diskette in drive A.

③ At the A> prompt type

DISKCOPY

④ Your PC displays the message:

> **Insert SOURCE diskette in drive A:**
> **Press any key to continue . . .**

⑤ Press any key to begin the copy operation. You see

> **Copying 40 tracks**
> **9 sectors/per track, 2 Side(s)**

⑥ The red drive light goes on and you hear a whirring sound. When the information on the diskette has been transferred into memory, you see

> **Insert TARGET diskette in drive A:**
> **Press any key to continue . . .**

⑦ Remove the application diskette.

⑧ Insert a blank diskette in the drive, close the drive door, and press any key to copy the application files onto this diskette.

Depending on the amount of memory available in your PC, you may have to repeat steps 4 through 7 more than once. If this is the case, DOS will tell you when to change diskettes.

⑨ Remove the backup copy of the application from the drive. Before you put it away, take time to label it. Return both diskettes to their protective sleeves, and store them in a safe place.

L oading an Application Program

After you have installed an application program, you load it whenever you want to use it. To load an application program

① Change the current directory to the application directory. The software manufacturer's installation instructions usually recommend a name for the application directory, but you can name it whatever you want.

② Type the program name. Refer to the software manufacturer's instructions for the correct program name.

③ Press ⏎.

Using an Application Program

All application programs are unique—even those intended for the same purpose work in different ways. Nonetheless, you will perform some typical operations, no matter what application you are using. We are going to introduce you to a few of these now.

Depending on your application, you will give commands, choose menu items, or use predefined function keys to perform the operations we will describe. For example, if you want to save a file, you might type the command Save in one application, press a function key labeled Save in another, or type a number corresponding to the menu choice Save in yet another. So our discussion of these operations is necessarily very general. Hopefully, with a few basic concepts in mind you will find it easier to master the applications themselves.

Entering and Saving Information

Often the first thing you'll do when you start using an application is enter the relevant information. It might be text for use with a word processor, financial information for a spreadsheet, or facts and figures for a database.

Although your information is displayed on the screen, it is only in your computer's memory for as long as you are working with it. If you leave the application program, reset your computer or turn off the power, your PC's memory will be wiped clean and you will lose all your information permanently. To avoid this, you have to store, or save, the information on your hard disk before you do any of the above things.

When you tell your PC to save some information, it does so by creating a file on the hard disk. You give the file a name before you save it so that next time you tell your PC to retrieve that information, it will know which file you are talking about. (Remember, file names must follow the rules discussed in Chapter 5.)

Most applications let you store files in directories other than the application directory or on a diskette instead of on your hard disk. You simply give the full path name when the application asks you to name the file. Although it is not necessary to store your information in a separate directory, it is a good idea. Storing information files separate from application files helps prevent accidentally writing over or deleting application files. Storing a backup version of a file on a diskette protects you against damage to your hard disk.

Retrieving the Information

Having saved a file, if you want to make changes or just check some information, you will have to retrieve the file from the hard disk or diskette. To do this, you give the command to read a file, and when the application asks which file, type its name. Include the full path name if the file is not in the current directory. If you forget the name of the file, use the application to list the file names in the directory where the file is stored.

Revising the Information

Once you have loaded the file, you can insert or delete text with your word processor, change the numbers in a spreadsheet report, or add some information to your database (not all at once, of course!).

Keep in mind that when you loaded the file, you made a *copy* and put it in your PC's memory. The original file is still safely stored on disk. The changes you make are *temporarily* in the computer's memory and don't become permanent until you save the new version of the file from memory onto disk again. There are three things you can do with the new version in your PC's memory:

- Don't save the new version at all. If you do not like the changes you have made, or if you just looked at the information but did not change it, there is no harm done. The original version is still on disk just as if you had never touched it.

- Replace the original version with the new version. If you want to overwrite the original version with the revised version, give the revised version the same name as the original version and save it on your hard disk.

- Save both versions. If you want to keep both the original version and the revised version, give the revised version a different file name if you are going to save it in the same directory, or save it on another directory.

Printing the Information

To get a paper copy, or *hard copy*, of your document, you will need to print it out. Before you start printing, always make sure your printer is connected, turned on, and has paper in it. Some printers also have an on-line button that you have to press before printing. (When a printer is *on-line*, it's ready to accept printing instructions from your PC.)

Depending on the application, you will give a print command, select Print from a menu, or press a Print function key. Then the program usually asks you to give the file name and supply some other details about how it should print the file.

Now for the work sessions. But first of all, here's a review of application programs in general.

Review

Running an application:

- Before you run an application program, you must install it on your hard disk.

- To load a program, first change the current directory to the application directory, and then type the program name.

Using an application:

- Operations are performed with commands that are typed directly, chosen from a menu, or selected using function keys.

- Entering, saving, retrieving, revising, and printing information are operations common to most applications.
- Information is saved as a file on disk. You need to supply the name of the file in order to work with it.

Chapter 9

Application Work Sessions

*F*eaturing

Creating a document with WordPerfect 5.1

Producing a spreadsheet with Lotus 1-2-3 (Versions 2.2 or 3.1)

*W*ordPerfect 5.1 Work Session

For some people, the main objective for buying a personal computer is to do word processing. Only later do they begin to explore their PC's many other capabilities.

WordPerfect is a very powerful word processing program. As it takes a little time to master all of its commands, we will not have time to tell you about even half of its capabilities. However, you are going to enter some text and play around with it a little, which will give you enough background to get started. For more complete coverage of WordPerfect, we recommend *Mastering WordPerfect 5.1* by Alan Simpson (SYBEX, 1990).

If you own a word processing program other than WordPerfect, don't skip over this work session thinking it a waste of your time. Reading through the exercises will give you an idea of how word processors work even though the commands for your program may be different.

We assume that you have already installed WordPerfect 5.1 on your hard disk. You should refer to the WordPerfect documentation for installation instructions. We've used Version 5.1 in these sessions. If you are working with an earlier version, the steps that follow will be exactly the same. However, some of the screen displays that you see might be slightly different from those that we illustrate.

Loading WordPerfect

The first step is to load WordPerfect. If you are using the DOS command line, make the WordPerfect directory the current directory. Type

WP

and press ←⎯.

If you are using the DOS 5 shell or Windows, display the appropriate directory or group and double-click the icon for the Word-Perfect program.

The WordPerfect Screen

When you first load WordPerfect, your screen clears except for some information in the lower-right corner; the cursor appears in the upper-left corner (see Figure 9.1). The cursor marks your typing position when you start entering text. If you're using a mouse, move or click the mouse and a pointer will appear on the screen.

WordPerfect Commands

With WordPerfect, you can use your PC's keyboard to select commands or you can use WordPerfect's pull-down menus. If you're using a mouse, you can use the mouse in combination with either the keyboard or the menus.

Wherever applicable, we will explain how to use the keyboard, menus, and the mouse. As you use WordPerfect more, you can decide which tool is easiest and quickest for you. You will probably end up using a combination of all three.

Figure 9.1: The WordPerfect screen

When you use the keyboard, you will use your PC's function keys and several other special keys to select commands. The keys have a different meaning depending on whether you use them alone or with the ⇧ (Shift) key, Alt key, or Ctrl key. WordPerfect comes with a template that fits around the function keys on your keyboard (see Figure 9.2). The keyboard template acts as a menu and reminds you of the function keys' uses. If you haven't already placed this template on your keyboard, do so now.

To turn on WordPerfect's pull-down menus, hold down the Alt key and type =. The menus will be displayed in a bar across the top of your screen. You can also display the menus by double-clicking a single-button mouse or clicking the right button on a two-button mouse.

You can select commands from the menus with the arrow keys on your keyboard. Use the left and right arrows (←, →) to move the cursor from menu to menu and use the up and down arrows (↑, ↓) to highlight a command in one of the menus.

You can also use the mouse to select commands. Click the mouse pointer on a menu and hold the mouse button down. Now scroll down the menu until the command that you want is highlighted. When you release the mouse button, the command will be executed.

WordPerfect® for IBM Personal Computers Delete to End of Ln/Pg — End/Pg Dn Delete Word — Backspace Go To — Home Hard Page — Enter ◆Margin Release — Tab Screen Up/Down — –/+ (num) Soft Hyphen — – Word Left/Right — ←/→ © WordPerfect Corp. 1988 TMENWP01/5.0 ISBN 1-55692-200-0	Shell Thesaurus Setup Cancel **F1**	Spell Replace ◆Search ◆Search **F2**	Screen Reveal Codes Switch Help **F3**	Move Block ◆Indent◆ ◆Indent **F4**	Ctrl Alt Shift	Text In/Out Mark Text Date/Outline List Files **F5**
	Tab Align Flush Right Center Bold **F6**	Footnote Math/Columns Print Exit **F7**	Font Style Format Underline **F8**	Ctrl Alt Shift	Merge/Sort Graphics Merge Codes Merge R **F9**	Macro Define Macro Retrieve Save **F10**	Reveal Codes **F11**	Block **F12**

Figure 9.2: The WordPerfect Keyboard Template

*E*ntering Text

The first thing that you will notice when you enter text is that you do not have to press ↵ at the end of a line. WordPerfect automatically wraps words around to the next line when you reach the right margin.

① Type the paragraph below to practice entering text. Don't worry about typing mistakes at this point. If you are compelled to correct an error, press the ← (Backspace) key once to delete each wrong letter and retype correctly.

Entering text with WordPerfect is just like using a typewriter, except that its much easier. Since words are automatically wrapped around at line endings, you don't have to worry about carriage returns until you get to the end of a paragraph.

② Now press ↵ twice to end the paragraph and leave a blank line before typing the next paragraph:

Editing text is the best part of using a word processor. You can go back and make changes to any part of the text with instant results.

*M*oving the Cursor

When you want to make a change to existing text, you have to start by moving the cursor to the point of the change. You can move the cursor by using the arrow keys or the mouse. The arrow keys are especially useful if you want to move the cursor a few words or lines away from its present position.

① Practice using the arrow keys to move up (↑), down (↓), right (→), and left (←) through the text that you just entered.

② You can skip a whole word at a time, either forward or backward through your text. Hold down the Ctrl key and press → to move the cursor to the right one word at a time. Hold down Ctrl and press ← to move the cursor to the left one word at a time.

If you want to move the cursor to a new paragraph or to a location a few pages away from its current position, using the mouse can make this a very quick step.

① Practice using the mouse to move the cursor through the text you entered. Position the mouse pointer in the text and click the mouse to move the cursor to that location.

*I*nserting Text

One of the advantages of using a word processor is that you can insert text anywhere you want within a document.

① To insert an extra phrase in the second paragraph, begin by moving the cursor to the *c* of the word *changes*:

Editing text is the best part of using a word processor. You can go back and make c̲hanges to any part of the text with instant results.

② Now type the phrase *all kinds of* (including the space after the last word).

③ Press any arrow key. That line and those that follow wrap around the right margin.

Editing text is the best part of using a word processor. You can go back and make all kinds of changes to any part of the text with instant results.

Deleting Text

You can delete text one character at a time, a word at a time, or a line at a time, using the keyboard or the pull-down menus. You can also delete whole blocks of text, but that's getting a bit fancy for this short work session. Let's delete a few characters first. This is easily done by using the ⟵ (Backspace) key.

① The ⟵ (Backspace) key deletes one character at a time to the left of the cursor, so you must begin by moving the cursor to the right of the deletion point. Use the arrow keys or the mouse to move the cursor to the space that follows the word *using* in the first paragraph you entered.

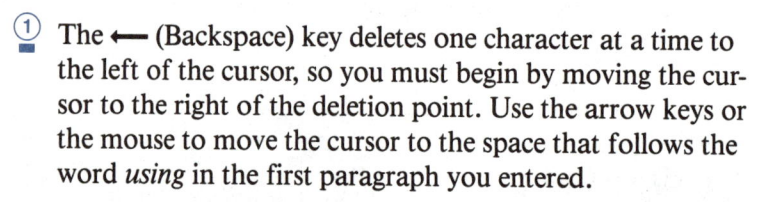

Entering text with WordPerfect is just like using_a typewriter, except that it's much easier. Since words are automatically wrapped around at line endings, you don't have to worry about carriage returns until you get to the end of a paragraph.

② Press ⟵ until the word *using* is deleted (that's six times; including the space before the word).

Entering text with WordPerfect is just like a typewriter, except that it's much easier. Since words are automatically wrapped around at line endings, you don't have to worry about carriage returns until you get to the end of a paragraph.

③ Now move the cursor in any direction. WordPerfect readjusts the lines in the paragraph so that they fit the margin.

Entering text with WordPerfect is just like a typewriter, except that it's much easier. Since words are automatically wrapped around at line endings, you don't have to worry about carriage returns until you get to the end of a paragraph.

You can also delete the character under the cursor. Press Del. The character that was to the right of the cursor moves underneath it.

Of course, it would have been easier to delete the word *using* all at once. Let's try this out on a word in the second paragraph that you typed.

① Move the cursor to the *u* of the word *using*.

Editing text is the best part of underline{u}sing a word processor. You can go back and make all kinds of changes to any part of the text with instant results.

② Hold down the Ctrl key and press ← (Backspace) to delete the entire word.

Editing text is the best part of a word processor. You can go back and make all kinds of changes to any part of the text with instant results.

Do you want to try deleting a whole line? Let's eliminate the line at the end of the first paragraph.

① Begin by moving the cursor to the beginning of the line to be deleted.

Entering text with WordPerfect is just like using a typewriter, except that it's much easier. Since words are automatically wrapped around at line endings, you don't have to worry about underline{c}arriage returns until you get to the end of a paragraph.

② Hold down the Ctrl key and press End. WordPerfect deletes from the cursor position to the end of the line.

Entering text with WordPerfect is just like using a typewriter, except that it's much easier. Since words are automatically wrapped around at line endings, you don't have to worry about

If you position the cursor within the line instead of at the beginning, WordPerfect deletes only the material from that point to the end of the line.

You can also delete a section of text by highlighting it with the mouse pointer, then pressing Del. In this exercise, you will delete a single line of text, but you may find this technique most useful when deleting larger sections of text.

① Move the cursor to the *a* in the word *at* in the first paragraph.

Entering text with WordPerfect is just like using a typewriter, except that it's much easier. Since words are automatically wrapped around at line endings, you don't have to worry about

② Hold down the left mouse button and drag the mouse pointer across the last line of text in the paragraph. WordPerfect highlights the selected text.

Entering text with WordPerfect is just like using a typewriter, except that it's much easier. Since words are automatically wrapped around at line endings, you don't have to worry about

③ WordPerfect displays this blinking message in the lower-left corner of the screen:

Block on

④ Press Del. WordPerfect displays this prompt at the bottom of the screen:

Delete Block? No (Yes)

⑤ Type Y or click Yes to delete the line of text.

⑥ The paragraph now appears like this:

Entering text with WordPerfect is just like using a typewriter, except that it's much easier. Since words are automatically wrapped around

Typing Over Text

You might sometimes want to go back and type over existing text (in effect, inserting new text and deleting old text at the same time). To do this, you press the Ins key to change from Insert to Typeover mode. When you begin, WordPerfect is in Insert mode, and text that you type is inserted before the cursor. In Typeover mode, you type over text beneath and to the right of the cursor.

① First, move the cursor to the first letter of the word that you want to type over, in this case the *r* of the word *results* in the second paragraph.

Editing text is the best part of using a word processor. You can

go back and make all kinds of changes to any part of the text with instant results.

② Press the Ins key to change from Insert mode to Typeover mode. On the bottom-left corner of the screen you see the message:

Typeover

WordPerfect expects that you'll be using Insert mode most of the time, so it displays a message only when you are in Typeover mode.

③ Type the new word *success* over the old word *results*.

Editing text is the best part of using a word processor. You can go back and make all kinds of changes to any part of the text with instant success.

④ Now press Ins again to return to Insert mode.

Saving the Document

When you have entered your text and made any necessary revisions, you will want to save the document for future use. It is a good idea to save documents in a separate directory from your WordPerfect program files. If you need instructions for creating a directory, see the documentation for your operating system. For this exercise, you should save the document in the root directory.

① Press F10 or select the Save command from the File menu. At the bottom of the screen, you see the message:

Document to be Saved:

② Name the file **PRACTICE** and save it in your root directory instead of the WordPerfect (current) directory by typing

\PRACTICE

③ Press ↵ to save the file. You see the message

Saving C:\PRACTICE

Printing the Document

If you have a printer that is connected to your PC, you can print the document to see what it looks like on paper. Before you do this, be sure that your printer is turned on and has paper in it.

① Hold down the Shift key and press F7 or select the Print command from the File menu. You see the Print and Options menus on the screen (see Figure 9.3). For this exercise, you will use only the Print menu.

When WordPerfect commands have additional options or they need more information, you see a menu. You select one of the options in the menu by typing its number or the highlighted letter in the option name. You can always type 0 to go back to whatever you were doing before you entered the command.

② Type 1 or F to print the full document.

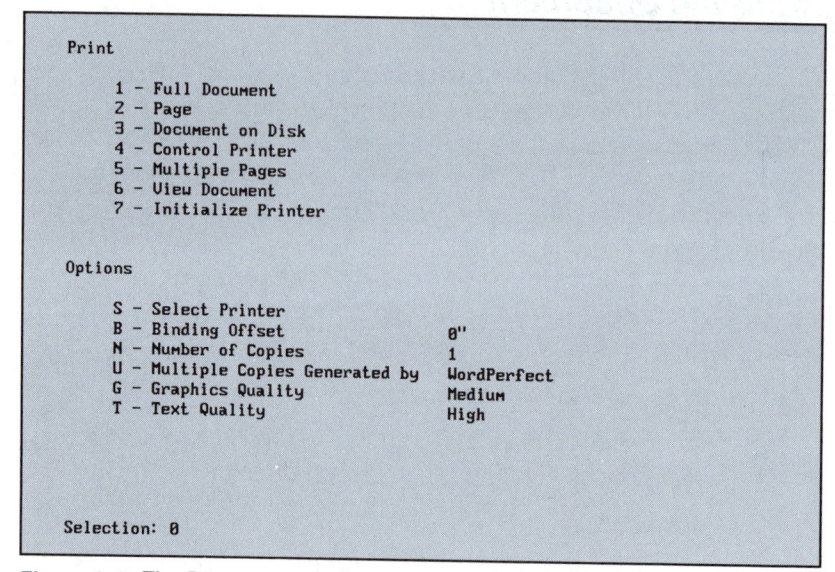

```
Print

    1 - Full Document
    2 - Page
    3 - Document on Disk
    4 - Control Printer
    5 - Multiple Pages
    6 - View Document
    7 - Initialize Printer

Options

    S - Select Printer
    B - Binding Offset                    0"
    N - Number of Copies                  1
    U - Multiple Copies Generated by      WordPerfect
    G - Graphics Quality                  Medium
    T - Text Quality                      High




Selection: 0
```

Figure 9.3: The Print and Options menus

Your printer should begin printing the document. If it doesn't, don't enter the print command again. Instead, reread your installation documentation and printer information to make sure that you installed WordPerfect correctly for your printer.

Clearing the Screen

Now that you've printed the PRACTICE document, what if you want to begin a new document? You simply clear the screen and begin typing the new document.

① Press F7 or select the Exit command from the File menu. WordPerfect asks whether you want to save the current document. The Y at the end of the prompt indicates that the default response (if you press ↵) is *Yes*. You can also press Y for *Yes* or N for *No*.

Save Document? Yes (No)

② Because you already saved the document, type N for *No*. WordPerfect asks whether you want to exit the program.

Exit WP? No (Yes)

③ Press ↵ to accept N for No. WordPerfect clears the screen.

Leaving WordPerfect

You have learned the basics of WordPerfect. As you can see, word processors are easy to use. Let's leave WordPerfect and experiment with a spreadsheet program.

① Press F7 or select the Exit command from the File menu. WordPerfect asks whether you want to save the current document:

Save Document? Yes (No)

(2) To save the document, type Y or click the mouse pointer on the Y, and give WordPerfect a file name. To leave Word-Perfect without saving the document, type N. WordPerfect asks whether you want to exit the program.

Exit WP? No (Yes)

(3) Press Y to answer *Yes*.

Listing the Files

If you want proof that your file is intact, list the files in the root directory. Your document should show up as

PRACTICE

unless, of course, you called it by a different name.

Lotus 1-2-3 Work Session

Of all the applications available, spreadsheets are one of the most popular. Lotus 1-2-3 from Lotus Development Corporation is currently the best-seller in the field. Moreover, it is easy to learn! If you have a copy of Lotus 1-2-3, you can sit down at your PC to complete the work session that follows. By going through the step-by-step instructions, you will create a simple report.

Although this work session is designed specifically for Lotus 1-2-3, all spreadsheets are remarkably similar. Therefore, it is worth reading through this work session, even if you do not have Lotus 1-2-3, to get some idea of how a spreadsheet works. Though the commands that are given are specific to 1-2-3, we have tried to make our discussion general enough to apply to any spreadsheet program.

Furthermore, you can use this work session with either version of 1-2-3 that is currently available on the market (Versions 2.2 and 3.1). Wherever applicable in the exercises, we note any differences between the two versions.

To run Version 3.1, your computer must have an 80286 or later CPU (80386, 80486) and at least one megabyte of RAM. The program will perform better if your CPU is 80386 or 80486 and if you have more than one megabyte of RAM.

We do not presume that in one short section we can tell you all about Lotus 1-2-3. We just want to give you the necessary steps to produce a simple report without going into all the whys and wherefores of every step. There are many other sources of information to supplement the exercise that you will do here. The tutorial and reference manual that come with the program will help a lot. We also recommend *The ABCs of Lotus 1-2-3 Release 2.2* by Chris Gilbert and Laurie Williams (SYBEX, 1989).

We assume that you have already installed 1-2-3 on your hard disk. You should refer to the program documentation for installation instructions.

Loading 1-2-3

The first step is to load 1-2-3. If you are using the DOS command line, make the 1-2-3 directory the current directory. Type

123

and press ↵.

If you are using the DOS 5 shell or Windows, display the appropriate directory or group and double click the icon for the 1-2-3 program.

The 1-2-3 Worksheet

The top, left-hand portion of the worksheet is always displayed on your screen after you load the program (see Figures 9.4 and 9.5). The entire worksheet is too large to fit on the screen all at once, so what you see is just a small part of it. However, special commands and the cursor-movement keys let you look at any part that you want.

The worksheet consists of

- **Columns**, which are identified by letters across the top. There are 256 columns in all, labeled A through IV. Each column is nine characters wide when you begin.

- **Rows**, which are identified by the numbers down the left side. There are 8,192 rows.

- **Cells,** which are the intersections of columns and rows.
    - In Version 2.2 of 1-2-3, cells are identified by a column letter followed by a row number; for example, A1.
    - Cell addresses in Version 3.1 are identified by a worksheet label followed by a colon (:), then the column letter and row number. Version 3.1 lets you store multiple worksheets in a file, and each worksheet is labeled alphabetically. The one worksheet that you will create in this exercise is labeled A; an example cell address is A:A1.
- **The Cell Pointer**, which is a highlighted bar. The cell pointer is in cell A1 (A:A1) when you begin. You use the cell pointer to move around in the worksheet and enter information.
- **The Cursor**, which is a short line inside the cell pointer.
- **The Control Panel**, which is the space above the column labels. As you work, the control panel display changes to show current worksheet information, menus, and prompts.
- **The Mode Indicator**, which is in the upper-right corner of the control panel. It tells you what mode 1-2-3 is in or what function it is currently performing. When you begin, the indicator reads **READY**, to tell you that the program is ready for you to enter information or commands.
- **The Date-and-Time Indicator** (Version 2.2 only), which reports the current date and time. It appears in the lower-left corner when you begin.
- **The File-and-Clock Indicator** (Version 3.1 only), which reports the current date and time if the current worksheet is not part of a file. If you have saved the worksheet in a file, the indicator displays the name of the file.
- **The Status Indicator**, which tells you when certain 1-2-3 modes are active. For example, when you begin, it displays UNDO, to remind you that you can press the undo key (F4) to undo the effects of your most recent operation. The indicator appears at the bottom of the screen.

Application Work Sessions 163

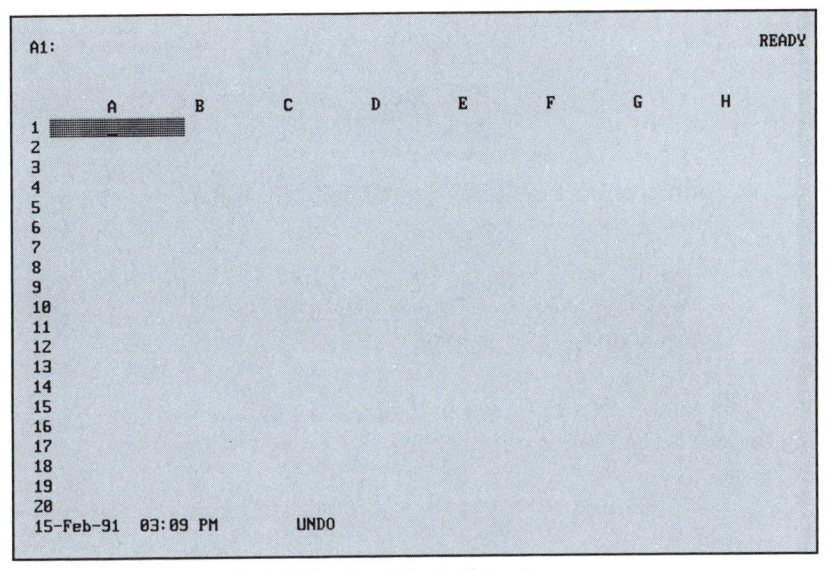

Figure 9.4: The Lotus 1-2-3 Version 2.2 worksheet

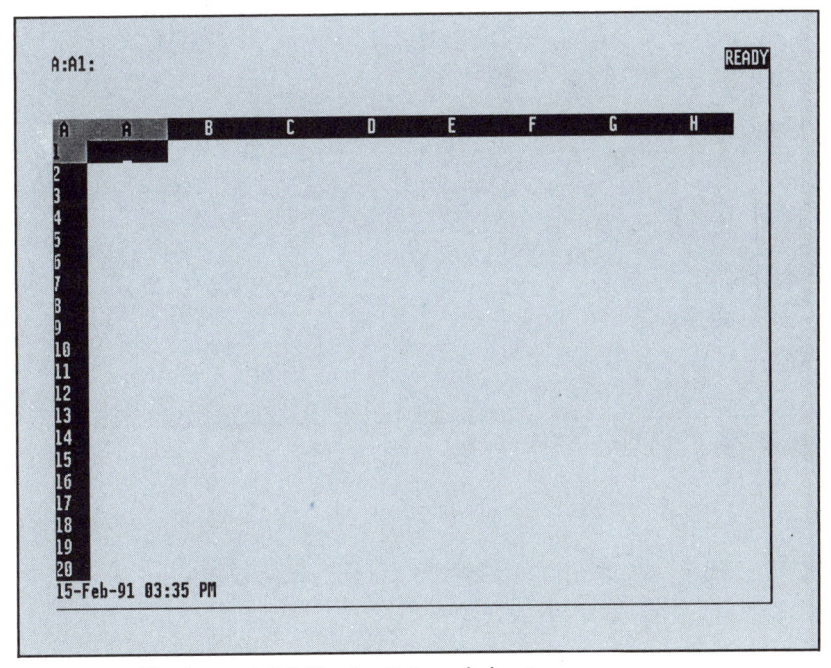

Figure 9.5: The Lotus 1-2-3 Version 3.1 worksheet

Creating a Report

When you create a 1-2-3 report, you can make two kinds of entries:

- **Labels** are usually titles for the column or row; for example, Sales, Expenses, and Profit.
- **Values** are numbers; for example, 1000, 300, and 7000, or formulas that perform calculations on the numbers in cells; for example, A:A2-A:B2.

The sample report shown in Figure 9.6 will let you practice making these different kinds of entries.

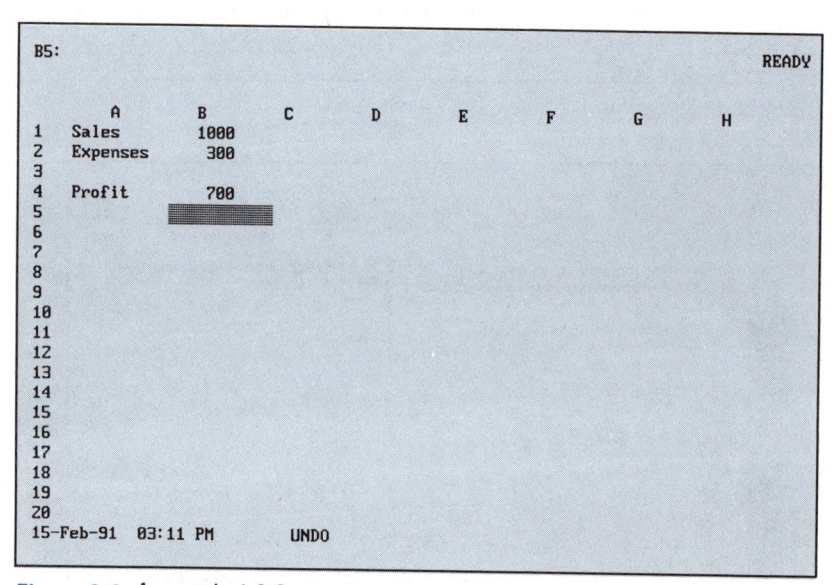

```
B5:                                                                    READY

          A         B         C         D         E         F         G         H
   1  Sales      1000
   2  Expenses    300
   3
   4  Profit      700
   5            ▓▓▓▓▓▓▓▓
   6
   7
   8
   9
  10
  11
  12
  13
  14
  15
  16
  17
  18
  19
  20
  15-Feb-91  03:11 PM        UNDO
```

Figure 9.6: *A sample 1-2-3 report*

There are always three steps involved in making an entry:

① Move the cell pointer to the cell that is to contain the entry.

② Type the entry.

③ Press ↵ or move to another cell to enter it in the worksheet.

Moving the Cell Pointer

When you want to enter a label or a value into the worksheet, you first have to move the cell pointer to the cell in which you want to type the information. You can use the arrow keys to move the cell pointer. The F5 function key, called the Goto key, lets you move the cursor directly to any cell on the worksheet.

① Practice using the arrow keys to move the cell pointer around in the worksheet. The → key moves the cursor to the right; the ← key moves it left and ↑ and ↓ move it up and down.

② Now you need to move the cursor back to cell A1 (A:A1) to begin creating our sample report. Press F5, and the control panel displays the prompt

Enter address to go to:

Notice that the control panel includes the current position of the cell pointer in the prompt. If you do not enter another cell name, the pointer stays where it is.

③ Type A1 and press ↵ to move the cell pointer to cell A1 (A:A1). You do not have to type the worksheet label in the cell address for Version 3.1 because you are working with only one worksheet.

Entering Labels

When you are ready to enter information into your worksheet, you will want to create labels, or headings, for that information. Once you have positioned the cursor in a cell, you can type in a label and then use the ↵ key or one of the arrow keys to enter it. Pressing the ↵ key enters the label in the worksheet and leaves the cursor in the current cell. Pressing an arrow key enters the label and moves the cursor to one of the adjacent cells.

① To move the cursor to cell A2 (A:A2), press ↓.

② To enter the label Sales in cell A2 (A:A2) and move the cell pointer down to cell A3 (A:A3), type

Sales

and press ↓.

Notice that the text appears on the second line of the control panel as you type. The label is not entered into the cell until you press the arrow key.

The mode indicator also changes from **READY** to **LABEL** as you type. This reminds you that you are in the process of adding a label.

③ To enter the label Expenses in cell A3 (A:A3) and move the cell pointer down to cell A4 (A:A4), type

Expenses

and press ↓.

④ To enter the label Income in cell A4 (A:A4) and leave the cell pointer in this cell, type

Income

and press ↵.

Entering Values (Numbers)

Now that your worksheet contains labels, you will enter values for each category. Use the same keys that you used for entering labels to move around the worksheet and enter values.

① To display the **Enter address to go to:** prompt in the control panel, press F5.

② To move the cell pointer directly to cell B2 (A:B2), type

B2

and press ↵.

③ To enter the number 1000 (no comma) in cell B2 (A:B2) and move the cell pointer down to cell B3 (A:B3), type

1000

and press ↓.

Notice the mode indicator changes from **READY** to **VALUE** as you type. It reminds you that you are in the process of entering a number (value).

④ To enter the number 300 in cell B3 (A:B3) and move the cell pointer down to cell B4 (A:B4), type

300

and Press ↓.

Entering a Formula

Lotus 1-2-3 will perform mathematical calculations on the values in the worksheet according to formulas that you enter.

① To enter a formula in cell B4 (A:B4) that tells 1-2-3 to subtract Expenses from Sales, type

+ B2 – B3

The + tells 1-2-3 that you are entering a formula. Notice that as you enter a formula, the mode indicator reads **VALUE**. The program is in the process of calculating the value that it will display in the cell.

② To perform the calculation and display the result, 700, in cell B4 (A:B4), press ⏎.

Now you know the basics of entering information into a Lotus 1-2-3 worksheet. Of course, you will be able to do a lot more when you have more experience using the program. However, you have already mastered creating a simple report.

The next important step is to save the report on your hard disk so that you can use it again. You must first learn how to use 1-2-3's menus.

Using Menus

All 1-2-3 commands are contained in the program's menus, which are displayed in the first and second lines of the control panel.

You can use one of two keys to turn on the menus: the slash key (/) or the less-than key (<).

When the menus are displayed, you see

- The **Main menu**, on the second line of the control panel.
- The **Menu pointer**, within the Main menu. When you first display the Main menu, the Menu pointer highlights the Worksheet command.
- A **submenu**, on the third line of the control panel. Because the Worksheet command is highlighted, the submenu displays a list of Worksheet commands.
- **MENU**, as the mode indicator.

Selecting a command from a 1-2-3 menu is easy. You can highlight the command with the mouse pointer and press ⏎, or you can simply type the first letter of the command you want to enter.

① Press the → key. The Menu pointer moves from Worksheet to Range, and the submenu displays Range commands.

② Press the → key again. The Menu pointer moves to Copy. Since Copy has no submenu of commands, the third line of the Control Panel displays an explanation of the Copy command.

③ Type **R**. The menu of Range commands is now displayed on the second line of the control panel.

You can use the Esc key to move backwards through the most recent sequence of commands that you entered.

① Press the Esc key. The Main menu is now displayed on the second line of the control panel, and the Range submenu returns to the third line.

② Press the Esc key again. The Main menu disappears, and 1-2-3 is ready for you to enter information in the worksheet.

Saving Your Report

Once you have entered all your information into a worksheet, you will want to save that worksheet as a 1-2-3 file.

① Press the slash key (/) or the less-than key (<) to display the Main menu.

② Select File. You see the File menu.

③ Select Save. 1-2-3 asks you to enter a file name:

In Version 2.2, the control panel displays the prompt

Enter name of file to save: C:\123

In Version 3.1, 1-2-3 displays the prompt

Enter name of file to save: C:\123\FILE0001.WK3

The prompt includes the complete path name for the current file (123 is our name for the 1-2-3 directory; you can name it anything that you like). When you type in the name of your file, it will replace the name provided in the prompt.

④ Type

Income

⑤ Press ↵ to save the file. The mode indicator changes to **WAIT** as 1-2-3 saves the file. After the file is saved, the mode indicator changes to **READY**. Your screen looks the same as it did before you displayed the Main menu.

Printing Your Report

If your PC is connected to a printer, you can print the worksheet that you just created.

① Press the slash key (/) or the less-than key (<) to display the Main menu.

② Select Print. You see the Print menu.

③ Select Printer to print your report.

If you have Version 2.2, the screen displays your current printer settings. In this exercise, you will work with the Range setting only.

Before you can print, you must tell 1-2-3 which cells that you want to print. You can print a rectangular block of one or more cells. This block is called a *range*. You identify a range with the addresses of the two most distant cells in the range separated by one or more periods. For example, A2.B4 names the range in which you have entered information. This is the range that you want to print.

④ Select Range. 1-2-3 asks you to

Enter Print range: B4

The prompt includes the current cell. If you do not name another range, 1-2-3 will print the current cell.

⑤ Type A2.B4 and press ⏎. The printer menu is displayed again.

If you are using Version 2.2, notice that the range section of the print settings display now contains the range you specified.

⑥ Select Go. The range you named prints.

If you are using Version 3.1, the status indicator displays PRT to remind you that 1-2-3 is printing a file.

⑦ Select Quit to leave the Printer menu.

Lotus 1-2-3 is now ready for you to enter new information in the worksheet.

*L*eaving 1-2-3

① Press the slash key (/) or the less-than key (<) to display the Main menu.

② Select Quit.

③ Select Yes.

Review

WordPerfect:

- Is a popular word processing program.
- Allows you to enter text and save it as a document.
- Provides automatic word wrap at line endings.
- Lets you go back and easily revise text.
- Allows you to insert, delete, and type over text; many other editing and formatting operations are possible.
- Save WordPerfect documents on disk if you want to use them later.

Lotus 1-2-3:

- Is a popular financial spreadsheet program.
- Consists of a worksheet of columns and rows that intersect to form cells for entering information.
- Allows you to make an entry by moving the cell pointer, typing the information, and entering it on the worksheet.
- Cell entries are labels, numbers, or formulas.
- Save Lotus 1-2-3 reports on disk if you want to use them later.

Part V

Beyond the Basics

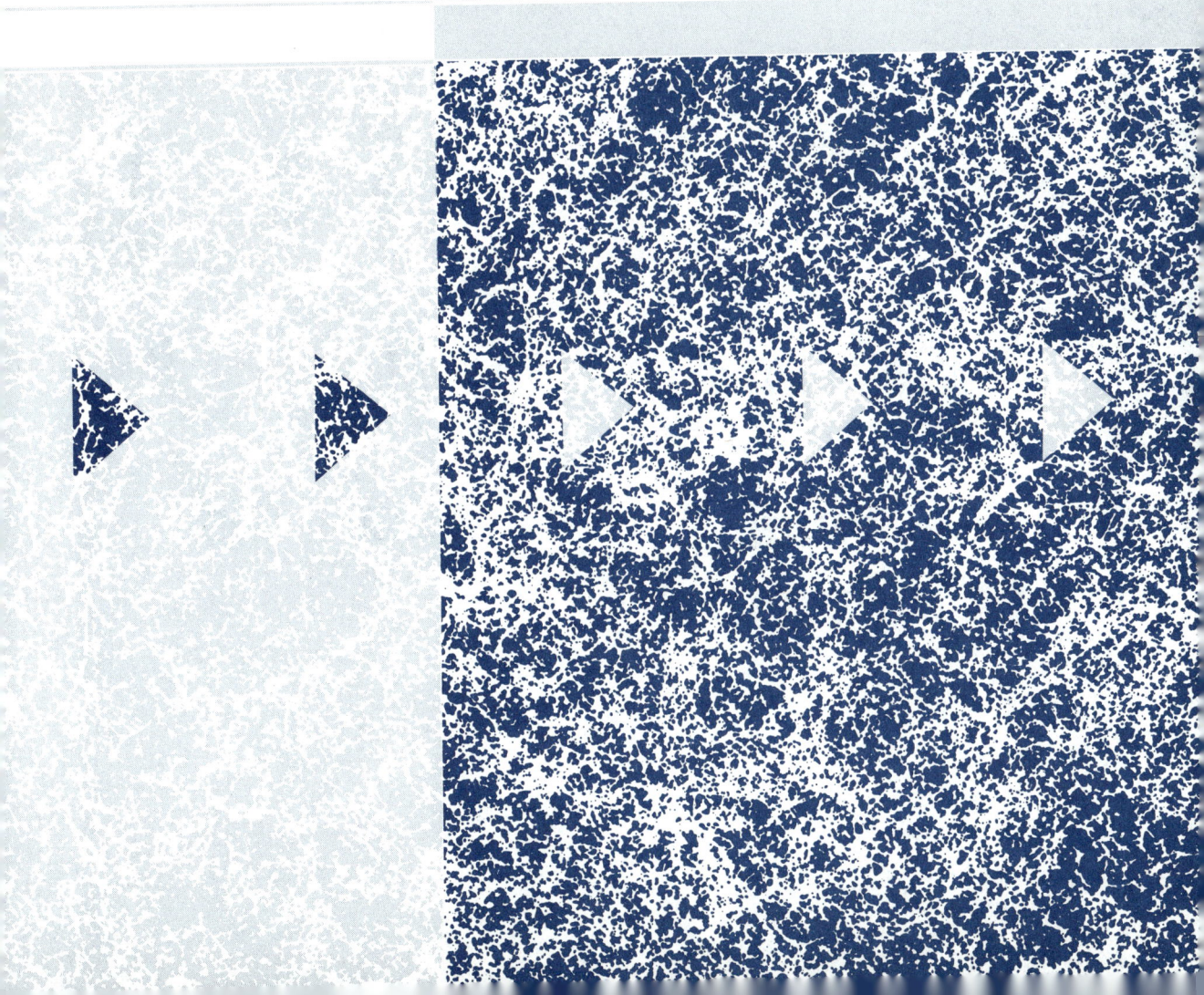

Chapter 10

Bells and Whistles: Optional Components

*F*eaturing

Extra disk drives

Printers

Additional memory

Color and graphics displays

Game control adapters

Plotters

Communications adapters

The PC is different things to different people. To some, it's a sophisticated typewriter—a word processor with a printer attached. To others, it's a fancy calculator that manages their financial affairs. Then there are those who write complex computer programs today and play video games tomorrow. The PC is a very versatile tool that can be customized for individual use by adding the application programs and bells and whistles that fit your particular needs.

Perhaps the basic PC is all you need, but you don't have to stop there! You can add printers and plotters, color and graphics, games and communications—whatever meets your needs or tickles your fancy.

Any of these additional options can be included in your initial PC purchase, or they can be added later as your needs change. The basic system unit has some empty spaces, called expansion slots, to accommodate adapters and printed-circuit boards for add-on options. The number of expansion slots is limited, so have someone check the space in your system unit before you purchase an option. Sorry—you can't have everything!

Some options are manufactured and supplied by your computer's manufacturer. Some are specially made by other companies to be compatible with the PC. Since your whole system has to work together, make sure a piece of equipment is compatible with your PC before you rush out to buy it.

This chapter gives you an overview of add-on options for the PC. If you are interested in adding options to your system, the first step is talk to your computer dealer to find out what is available. New products are constantly being developed and you will want to know what your choices are before making a purchase.

In addition, be sure you know what else is involved. Do you need special adapters or a specific amount of memory? Do you have to purchase cables and connectors separately? Take some time to check into all this ahead of time and you will be sure to end up with what you wanted.

Extra Disk Drives

In this book, we have assumed you are using a system with one hard disk and one diskette drive. One diskette and one hard disk drive are usually enough for one person, but you can add up to 26 drives (although managing so many drives is probably more trouble than it's worth). More likely, you may eventually replace your hard disk drive with one that has more storage space, or you may add a different type of diskette drive so that you can share information with others. For example, if a co-worker has a PC that uses 3.5-inch diskettes, you may want to add a 3.5-inch diskette drive to your system so that the two of you can easily share files.

Printers

For many people, a printer is not an option; it is an essential piece of equipment. If you will be doing word processing or producing any kind of report that needs to be on paper, you will certainly need a printer. There are three types of printers that are popular: laser printers, letter-quality printers, and dot-matrix printers.

Laser printers use technology similar to a photocopier to print one page at a time at high speed. They produce the highest quality text of the three types. With a laser printer, you can print text in a variety of sizes and styles. You can also print text and graphics on the same page. If you are using a desktop publishing program, a laser printer is essential.

Letter-quality print looks as though it comes from a typewriter and is produced in much the same way, with a cartridge ribbon and a print wheel. Like a typewriter element, the print wheel can be changed to produce many different typefaces. This kind of printer is used mostly with word-processing applications or wherever high-quality letters and reports are required.

Dot-matrix print is composed of small dots that give a more uneven appearance than letter-quality print. It's fine for many jobs—program listings, memos, and drafts—but it's not good for more formal business correspondence.

The major deciding factor between the three, then, is the quality of print you require. Other considerations are speed and price. Laser printer speed is measured in pages per minute. Letter-quality and dot-matrix printer speed is measured in characters per second. Printer speed varies greatly from printer to printer. In general, laser printers are the fastest and letter-quality printers are the slowest. Dot-matrix printers are usually the least expensive. However, the decision usually comes back to the issue of print quality.

Your printer will come with a printer cable and instructions for connecting it to your PC. For some printers, you may also have to have a special adapter installed in the system unit.

Additional Memory

The system unit of the PC includes a working memory which temporarily holds the program and information you are currently using. Your PC has at least 128 kilobytes of memory. Ours has 640 kilobytes. A kilobyte (*or K*) is around a thousand bytes, and you can think of a byte as approximately one character, so 640 K of memory gives you space for about 640 thousand characters of working information. Your PC may have even more memory than ours. Greater amounts of memory are measured in megabytes. One megabyte is around one thousand kilobytes.

If you work with large programs and information files you will need more memory than if you produce the odd report or memo. More memory increases the PC's ability to handle large jobs, and more is usually better. With word-processing programs, editing a large document goes faster if you have more memory since the whole document can fit in memory at one time. In addition, some application programs and other options specify the minimum amount of memory that your PC must have in order for you to run the program.

You buy your PC with as much memory as you think you will initially need. You can have more installed in the system unit later if your needs change. If you need more memory than your system unit can hold, you can purchase memory adapters to install in your PC.

Color and Graphics Displays

Perhaps you want to produce illustrations, bar charts, pie charts, and graphs. Or would you like to play video games? With a color or graphics display, you can do both. Graphics and color usually go hand-in-hand; you get color on the screen as well as graphics capabilities. However, for some word- processing and desktop publishing applications, you can get monochrome graphics displays that let you display different typefaces and artwork inside your written documents.

Although you use a color graphics display primarily for graphics applications, you can also use it with any other application. Usually, the quality of text on a color display is not as good as a monochrome display, so people who use their PCs mainly for word-processing prefer monochrome displays.

In addition to the color or graphics display, you will have to have a color or graphics monitor adapter installed in the system unit. Be sure that the display and the adapter are compatible.

Game Control Adapters

And since we mentioned games, you'll need a game control adapter if you want to play interactive games that use a joystick. If your computer's manufacturer doesn't offer joysticks, they can be purchased elsewhere and connected to the system unit with the game control adapter.

Plotters

A plotter is like a printer in that it gives you paper output, but there the similarity ends. A printer just prints; a plotter is an electronic artist. Instead of a print wheel, a plotter has colored pens (up to eight) that pick themselves up and move across the paper to write and draw. Plotters are used mainly with graphics applications to produce graphs and charts, as well as overhead transparencies and presentation aids.

To use a plotter with your PC, you may need to have a special adapter installed in the system unit.

Communications Adapters

Your keyboard and display allow you to communicate with your PC; a communications adapter allows your PC to communicate with other computers.

Computer communications is a wide-ranging area of technology that is constantly developing. It offers many different options. Some communications require the addition of a modem (electronic, telephone-like devices), some require that your computer be connected into a communications network, and others require special software programs. What computer communications can offer you will depend entirely on your particular situation, but some possibilities are

- Sending and receiving electronic mail messages
- Sending information across telephone lines
- Sharing information with other PC users
- Subscribing to public information services
  (more on these in Appendix C)

- Sharing access to a large central computer
- Using a printer or disk drive that is not even attached to your PC

Communications adapters also allow you to use other equipment such as plotters, letter-quality printers, and voice-recognition devices.

Chapter 11

Checklists: If Something Goes Wrong

*F*eaturing

Troubleshooting guide

When to ask for help

Despite the high quality and reliability of the PC itself and the care you take in using it, at some point something will go wrong. When your computer won't do what you want, it can be very frustrating, so this chapter gives you some pointers for getting out of trouble.

Most problems are caused by one of two things—either you have given the computer incorrect or incomplete instructions, or something really isn't working properly. Hard as it may be to take, the first of these is usually the case. It's worth taking the time to check on yourself before you bundle up your PC and send it off for repair. Even if you are not the culprit, your service person will be able to help you much better if you can be specific about the details of the problem.

Let's start with you. Ask yourself the questions in our *You* Checklist. Does this solve the problem? Don't be embarrassed; we all make these mistakes. Just correct the problem and try again.

If the first list is no help, go on to the *PC* Checklist, which gives typical trouble areas that you can check for yourself. Although some may sound obvious (*of course* the power is on), you never know who tripped over the power cord when your back was turned.

Your Checklist

- Did you get an error message? Look it up in the back of the appropriate reference manual and follow the recovery steps.
- Has DOS been installed on your hard disk? You cannot do anything until it is.
- Did you make a typing mistake? Correct the error and try again.
- Are you using the software correctly? Check the appropriate reference manual to be sure you are not confused about what you are trying to do.
- Are you looking for the file in the correct directory? Use the DIR command or the mouse to check the files in a directory.
- Are you using the correct diskette? Again, use the DIR command or the mouse to list the files.
- Does the path name need a drive identifier? If the file is not on the current drive, you need to precede the path name with the proper drive identifier.
- Does the file name have an extension? If it does, you have to use it.
- Has the diskette been formatted? You cannot store information on a new diskette until you format it.
- Are you using a defective diskette? Take the diskette out and examine it for chips, bumps, or scratches.
- Is the disk write-protected? Take it out and examine the write-protect notch or window.
- Have you inserted the diskette properly? Make sure it is inside the drive as far as it will go and the drive door is closed.
- Did you close the drive door properly? Open and close it just to be sure.

- When was the last time you cleaned the diskette drives? Honestly?
- Ask someone else to take a look. We're always the last ones to notice when we've made a mistake!

*P*C Checklist

- Turn off the system power and disconnect the power cord from the wall. Always do this before you start investigating cables and connections.
- Plug another appliance into the wall outlet to see if the outlet works.
- Check that the cable connections for the keyboard and display are securely attached to the system unit. Also check the PC end of the power cord.
- Turn the contrast and brightness controls all the way to the right. If they have been turned down accidentally, you may not be able to see anything on the display. You can adjust them again later.
- Plug the power cord back into the wall and turn on the system power. The PC will run through its self test, load DOS, and ask you to enter the date and time.
- If DOS does not load properly, refer to your operations manual for more help on diagnosing the problem.
- Ask for help. Two heads are almost always better than one.

*S*ervice

If all else fails, you are going to need help from a professional service organization. Find your warranties and check your service contract. Different types of PCs come with different warranties. Most dealers also offer extended service contracts. If your PC belongs to your company, check to see if they have their own service arrangements.

Make a note of exactly how the problem occurred and any error messages you received. This is important diagnostic information.

For more information, refer to the service information in your operations manual.

Appendix A

Putting It All Together

This appendix is for those of you who have just arrived home with your brand new IBM PC/AT. It tells you everything you need to know to put your PC together. We will help you choose a good working location and unpack the shipping containers, and then go through the steps for connecting the components.

If you have a different kind of PC, you use a similar procedure. Before you assemble your PC, you may want to read through this chapter for some general guidelines, and then read the specific instructions that came with your PC.

Again, we are assuming that your computer dealer has set up your hard disk and installed DOS on it. If this is not the case, ask your dealer or your service person to do so. Although there are instructions for setting up your hard disk in your DOS reference manual, it is best to have an experienced person do it for you.

Before you begin, find a small, flat-blade screwdriver, and notice where there are grounded (3-pin) power outlets to plug your PC into when you are ready to go.

Choosing a Location

You need to take some important facts into account when deciding where to set up your PC:

① Don't pick a place where you will be sitting with your back to a light. The glare of the light on the screen will make it difficult (sometimes impossible) to work.

② Think about the cables and power cord. Will they be tucked out of the way or will you be inviting someone to trip over them if you put your computer here? Move the PC closer to the wall outlet if necessary.

③ Think about the back of the machine as well as the front. At some point, you will probably need to get at the rear panel. Will it be accessible without a major furniture upheaval?

④ Give the PC enough room. The system unit is quite deep and should not be balanced on the edge of a narrow desk. Most people put the keyboard in front of the system unit, so allow space for that, too. If you prefer, you can set the keyboard to one side.

⑤ Give yourself enough room—more than the PC itself occupies. When you start working, you will need space for manuals, papers, diskettes, and perhaps a printer. Choose your working location with this in mind so that things will go smoothly later.

Unpacking the System Unit

① The system unit is in the large, heavy box. Turn the container right side up, cut the binding tape, and open the box.

② In the cardboard tray on top of the box, you will find the following items:

- An inventory checklist for each item. Since the warranty is printed on the back of the checklists, keep these in a safe

Putting It All Together **191**

place for now and insert them in your operations manual later.

- Power cord. Keep this handy—you'll need it soon.
- Two manuals: *Guide to Operations* and *BASIC*. The *Guide to Operations* manual tells you all about operating your PC; the *BASIC* manual tells you how to use the BASIC programming language to program your PC.
- A plastic bag containing some fact sheets and an IBM customer response card. Put these with the checklists for now and read and complete them later.

③ Having removed these items, take out the cardboard tray.

④ Lift out the system unit. It is tightly packed and quite heavy, so go carefully. Keep all the packing materials in case the system has to be shipped again.

⑤ Take the system unit out of the plastic bag and place it on a flat surface in your chosen location. You will need access to the rear and enough room to work.

⑥ Open the diskette drive door(s) and remove the cardboard inserts.

⑦ Check that the power is off. If you are facing the front of the system unit, the power switch is on the right side of the unit towards the back.

Connecting the Keyboard

① Open the long, flat box that contains the keyboard. Take out the inventory checklist/warranty and keep it in a safe place. Put it in the operations manual later.

② Remove the polystyrene packing material, lift out the keyboard, and take it out of its plastic bag. Keep all packing materials.

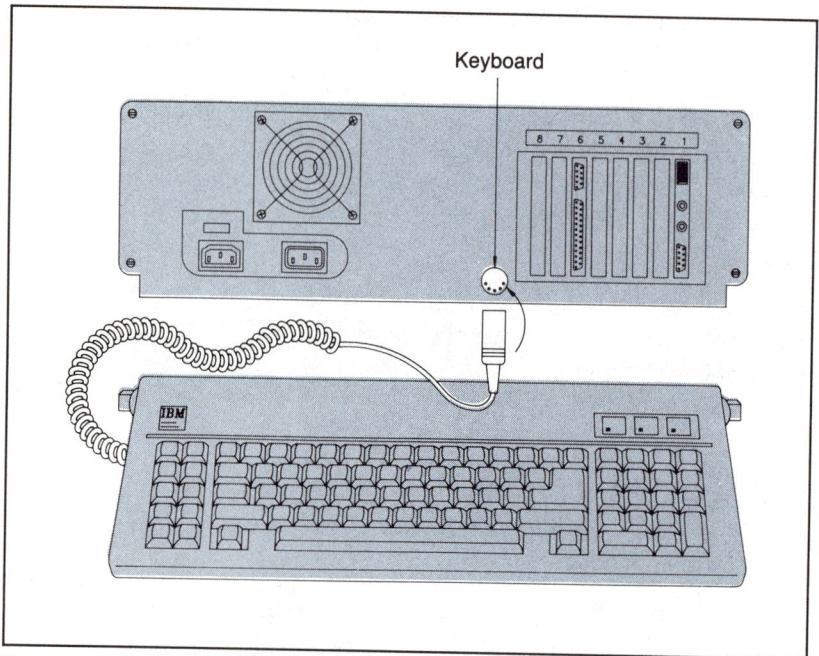

Figure A.1: Connecting the Keyboard

③ Place the keyboard in front of the system unit. Connect the keyboard cable to the back of the system unit (see Figure A.1). Make sure you push the cable connector on firmly.

Connecting the Display

① Turn the display container right side up, cut the binding tape, and open the container.

② Take out the inventory checklist/warranty and keep it in a safe place. Put it in the operations manual later.

③ Remove the display. Like the system unit, it is tightly packed, so you will have to struggle a bit. Take off the packing materials and plastic bag and store them with the others.

④ Put the display on top of the system unit.

⑤ Take the plastic bag off the cables on the back of the display.

⑥ Connect the display cables to the back of the system unit (see Figure A.2). Push both cable connectors on firmly, then tighten the retaining screws on the right-hand connector.

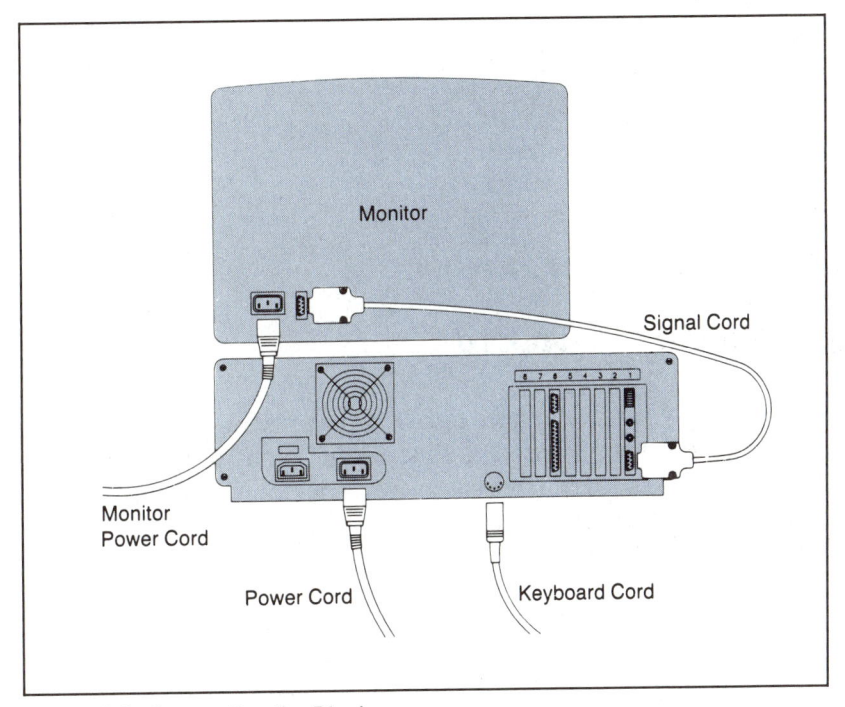

Figure A.2: *Connecting the Display*

Connecting the Power Cord

① Connect one end of the power cord to the back of the system unit (see Figure A.3).

② Plug the other end of the power cord into a grounded wall outlet.

APP. A

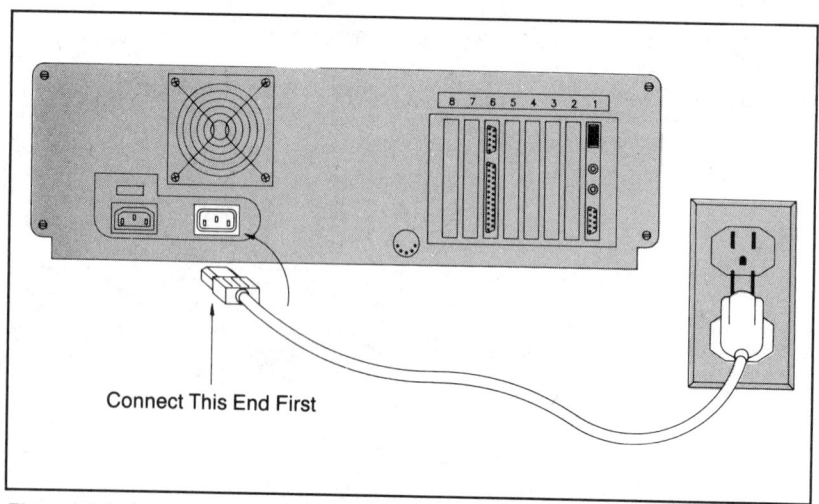

Figure A.3: Connecting the Power Cord

Adjusting the Keyboard

The keyboard is designed to be level or to tilt and is adjusted with the knobs on the top corners. Squeeze the knobs in and turn them toward you to tilt the keyboard, away from you to make it level (see Figure A.4). Try it both ways so that you can decide which feels best for you.

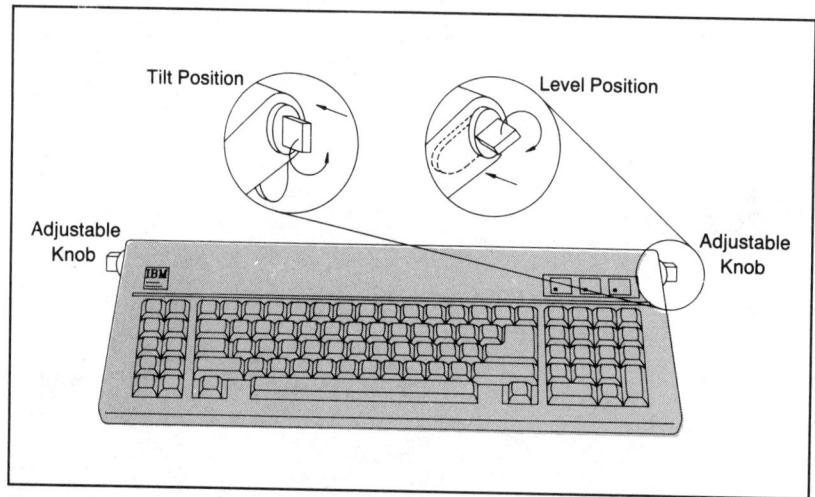

Figure A.4: Adjusting the Keyboard

That's it! Take a minute to make sure your PC is set up in a good location, then go back to Chapter 1 to find out what all these components do, or to Chapter 2 where we tell you how to turn on the power and start using your PC.

Appendix B

Glossary

Backup

A backup is a duplicate copy of a file or diskette. When you make such a copy, you are *doing a backup*. Back up a hard disk using the DOS BACKUP command; back up a diskette using the DOS DISK-COPY command; back up a file using the DOS COPY command. You can also purchase special backup programs for use with your hard disk.

Bit

Short for Binary Digit. That tells you a lot, doesn't it! Well, we could go on about binary digits being 0 and 1 and computers operating on ON/OFF signals where ON is 1, and OFF is 0, but, honestly, would you be any the wiser? You might want to remember that there are eight bits in a byte, but then again, you might not.

Boot

When you load the operating system, DOS, you are *booting* your computer. Loading DOS by turning the power on is a *hard (or cold) boot;* resetting is a *soft (or warm) boot*.

Bug

Anything that makes the computer or its software stop working as planned. The story goes that an insect trapped inside an early computer caused it to malfunction; little did that insect know it was headed for immortality!

Byte

The unit of measurement for computer storage and memory. A byte can store about one character of information. There are eight bits in a byte.

Chip

Also called a silicon chip. This tiny sliver of silicon, containing incredibly complex circuits, is the heart and soul of your computer and the single technological advance that shrank it to desktop size.

CPU

Short for central processing unit. It is the device in the system unit of your PC where information is processed. Also known as a microprocessor.

Crash

A complete malfunction of your computer, much worse than a bug. Originally meant that the read/write head inside the diskette drive had crashed into the disk, but has now become a generic term for any major breakdown.

CRT

Short for cathode ray tube. The tube itself is a television tube that allows information to be shown on the display screen, but the term is used to refer to computer terminals and displays that use CRTs.

Daisy Wheel

The kind of print wheel used in many letter-quality printers. It has a central hub and lots of spokes with printable characters on the ends. Looks *something* like a daisy.

Data

Hardly a computer term anymore. Everyone gathers and processes data these days. Really just means information.

Database

A collection of files that are grouped together because they have something in common. They can be sorted and accessed selectively and thus form valuable sources of information. When you receive junk mail, chances are your name has been pulled out of a large computer database.

Debug

Correcting a hardware or software error—getting the bugs out—is debugging.

Default

Something the computer assumes unless you tell it otherwise.

Downtime

If your system crashes, it will be out of action, or *down*, for a while. If the crash occurred at 1:45 pm and the system is not repaired until 4:03 pm the same day, the downtime was 2 hours and 18 minutes.

Fixed Disk

Another name for hard disk.

Floppy Disk

Another name for a diskette. Sometimes just called a *floppy*.

Flowchart

A sort of road map to a computer program. Programmers design a flowchart to help them write a program. It tells them what should follow what and where to go if a particular event occurs.

Gigabyte

2^{40} bytes (1,099,511,627,776 bytes). Gigabyte is usually abbreviated Gb.

Hard Copy

A printed paper copy of anything your computer produces, from a computer program listing to a word-processing document.

Head

A small magnetic device inside a disk drive that reads and writes information on disks.

Input

Anything you put into your computer—commands, programs, instructions. Your input tells the computer what to do.

Interactive

When you give your computer an instruction and it responds, you are interacting with each other. Most application programs are interactive.

Interface

Hardware or software that allows communication between your computer and you or other devices. For example, a printer interface lets you transfer information from your PC to a printer.

Kilobyte

One kilobyte is 2^{10} bytes (1,024 bytes). Kilobyte is usually abbreviated K or Kb.

Kludge

Everybody has their own definition of this term. For us, it's hardware or software that has been put together sloppily. It works, but nobody is sure why. Your PC is *not* a kludge.

Laser Printer

A high-speed printer that prints one full page of high-quality text and/or graphics at a time. Used with desktop publishing and other applications where printer quality is important. Often shared by PC users.

Line Feed

To advance by one line. Most printers have a line feed button that you press to move the paper up by one line.

Line Printer

A high-speed printer capable of printing an entire line at a time. Used with large, shared computers rather than individual personal computers.

Logged Drive

Another way of saying the current or default disk drive.

Megabyte

One megabyte is 2^{20} bytes (1,048,576 bytes) and is abbreviated Mb.

Memory

The part of the computer that stores programs and information needed to perform the current operation. There are different kinds of memory (see RAM and ROM).

Microcomputer

A complete, small, computer system, like your PC.

Microprocessor

See CPU.

Mouse

A small, device that sits to the side of your keyboard. You move a pointer on the display by moving the mouse on your desk. You press one of the mouse's buttons to select objects or commands.

Network

A group of interconnected computers that can share, send, and receive information among themselves.

Operating Environment

A program that changes the way you interact with your PC. Instead of requiring you to type DOS commands to communicate with your PC, most operating environments let you select commands with a mouse and view files through windows on your display.

Output

What your computer comes up with after acting on your input. The output may be displayed on the screen, stored on a disk, or printed, depending on your instructions.

Peripheral

Any additional equipment you attach to your computer. Printers and disk drives are typical peripherals.

RAM

Random access memory—the part of the computer's memory that temporarily holds your program and instructions while you are working with them. When you turn the computer off, RAM loses whatever it contains.

Read a Disk

To copy information from a disk into the computer's memory. You can't use the information stored on a disk until it has been read into memory.

Response Time

The interval between you telling the computer to do something and it acting on your instructions. The shorter the better.

ROM

Read only memory—the part of the computer's memory that holds information permanently. With your PC, BASIC is in ROM and is stored there at all times, even when you turn the PC off.

Utility

Software used for regularly performed operating system operations such as managing or recovering files. Several steps are combined to carry out a complete operation with only one instruction from you—makes your life easier.

Window

An area on your screen that displays information. Normally, you can move and change the size of a window. Some application programs let you work with multiple files at once by displaying them in different windows. Operating environments use windows to let you work with more than one application.

Write to a Disk

To copy information from the computer's memory onto a disk. Keeps a permanent copy on disk for future use.

Appendix C

Resources

Magazines

There are dozens of magazines that can help you to learn more about your PC. Here we list several general-purpose magazines. You might be able to get samples from your computer dealer or at your local bookstore. In addition, software manufacturers often send newsletters to registered application users. These newsletters might give you tips for using the program more efficiently, profile other users, or describe new products.

Other good sources of information are the professional societies to which you belong. They can refer you to magazines for your particular profession. For example, there are magazines aimed at personal computer users in the fields of medicine, law, and agriculture.

BYTE, McGraw-Hill Inc.

Monthly, $24.95/year

Send subscription inquiries to: BYTE Subscriptions, P.O. Box 550, Hightstown, NJ 08520. Phone (800) 232-2983; outside US (609) 426-7070.

For the experienced computer user. Articles and information are technical in nature and are intended for people who want to know how their computer is put together and what makes it work.

> *Computer Shopper,* Ziff-Davis Publishing Co.
>
> Monthly, $29.97/year
>
> Send subscription inquiries to: Computer Shopper, P.O. Box 52568, Boulder, CA 80322. Phone (800) 274-6384.

For all microcomputer users. Software and hardware reviews, new product information, book reviews, bulletin board and user-group information.

> *Family and Home Office Computing,* Scholastic, Inc.
>
> Monthly, $19.97/year
>
> Send subscription to Family and Home Office Computing, P.O. Box 51334, Boulder, CO 80322-1334. Phone (303) 447-9330.

For people who use their computers at home. Includes ideas for using computers in a home office, hardware and software reviews, features on computers for education and entertainment, and tutorials.

> *InfoWorld,* InfoWorld Publishing, Inc.
>
> Weekly, Free of charge to qualified buyers of microcomputers and related products. To all others, $110/year.
>
> Send subscription inquiries to: InfoWorld, P.O. Box 3014, Northbrook, IL 60065. Phone (800) 457-7866.

Software reviews, new product information, book reviews, computer literacy for the novice, industry reports.

> *Online Access,* Chicago Fine Print, Inc.
>
> Quarterly, $19.80/year
>
> Send subscription inquiries to: Subscription Services, Online Access, 2271 N. Lincoln Ave, Chicago IL 60614. Phone (312) 935-1400.

For PC users interested in learning to use online services and commercial databases. Includes news, reviews, and guides to services.

PC Computing, Ziff-Davis Publishing Company

Monthly, $24.97/year

Send subscription inquiries to: PC Computing, P.O. Box 54093, Boulder, CO 80322. Phone (800) 525-0643; outside U.S. (303) 447-9330.

For a business audience. Includes hardware and software information, new product information.

PC Magazine, Ziff-Davis Publishing Company

Biweekly, $44.97/year

Send subscription inquiries to: PC Magazine, P.O. Box 54093, Boulder, CO 80322. Phone (303) 447-9330.

For a general audience. Includes hardware and software information, software reviews, and general news.

PC WEEK, Ziff-Davis Publishing Company

Weekly, $160/year

Send subscription inquiries to: Customer Service Department, PC WEEK, P.O. Box 1770, Riverton, NJ 08077. Phone (609) 461-2100.

For business users of microcomputers. Includes product information, reviews, and business news.

PC World, PCW Communications, Inc.

Monthly, $29.90/year

Send subscription inquiries to: PC World Subscription, Subscriber Services, P.O. Box 55029, Boulder, CO 80322-5029. Phone (800) 234-3498.

For a general audience. Includes hardware and software information, software reviews, personality profiles, user-group and bulletin board updates.

>*Publish!,* PCW Communications, Inc.
>
>Monthly, $39.90/year
>
>Send subscription inquiries to: Subscriber Services, P.O. Box 55400, Boulder, CO 80322. Phone (800)274-5116 or (303) 447-9330 in Colorado.

For users of desktop-publishing programs. Includes news, hardware and software reviews, tips, and page makeovers.

Information Services

The widespread use of computers, especially personal computers, has created an information explosion. More facts and figures are available now than ever before. Information can give you an advantage in business, in school, in planning your career, and in making purchase decisions for your home. With a small investment in a communications adapter and the software to use it, your PC can plug you into the information you need.

We discuss three types of information services in this section: public information services, database vendors, and electronic mail services. Because these services are continuously evolving, contact the vendors listed for current information.

Public Information Services

Public information services offer subscribers the latest news and information from a variety of sources. By subscribing to the service of your choice, you can turn your PC into an electronic newspaper, mail box, travel agent, and more. Public information services give you access to special interest group information, software, bulletin boards, electronic mail, online games, and the services of several database vendors (described in the next section).

CompuServe

CompuServe Information Service, Inc.

5000 Arlington Centre Blvd.

Columbus, OH 43220

(800)848-8990 or (614)457-8650 in Ohio and outside the contiguous U.S.

Delphi

General Videotext Corporation

3 Blackstone Street

Cambridge, MA 02139

(800)544-4005 or (617)491-3393 in Massachusetts

GEnie

General Electric Information Services

401 N. Washington Street

Rockville, MD 20850

(800)638-9636

PeaceNet

IGC Networks

18 DeBoom St.

San Francisco, CA 94107

(415)442-0220

Database Vendors

Database vendors give you access to information. Usually the database is compiled by another firm, although database vendors sometimes compile their own databases. Some databases are available exclusively from one vendor, while others are available from virtually all vendors. Membership fees and rate schedules vary among vendors and their different products. Request more information from several database vendors before you sign up with one. Some databases are also available from the public information services described in the previous section.

BRS/After Dark

BRS/Colleague

BRS/Educator

BRS/Instructor

BRS/Morning Search

BRS/Search

BRS/Student

BRS Information Technologies

Maxwell Online, Inc.

8000 Westpark Dr.

McLean, VA 22102

(800)955-0906

BRS services give you access to over 150 databases. BRS/SEARCH and BRS/COLLEAGUE are the main systems. BRS/SEARCH is designed primarily for librarians and other information professionals, and BRS/COLLEAGUE is for healthcare professionals.

Data-Star

485 Devon Park Drive, Suite 110

Wayne, PA 19087

(800)221-7754 or (215)687-6777 in Pennsylvania

Data-Star provides European business information through over 250 databases. Subjects include business news, medicine, chemistry, engineering, and the environment.

DIALOG

DIALOG Business Connection (DBC)

The Knowledge Index (KI)

DIALOG Information Services, Inc.

3460 Hillview Avenue

Palo Alto, CA 94304

(800)334-2564

DIALOG gives you access to over 400 databases. DIALOG Business Connection offers the most business-oriented DIALOG databases in a menu-driven format. The Knowledge Index offers over 90 DIALOG databases at reduced rates after normal business hours.

Dow Jones News/Retrieval Service

P.O. Box 300

Princeton, NJ 08543-0300

(609)452-1511

Offers about 55 databases. Over half are produced by Dow Jones. Focuses on financial information, up-to-the-minute stock and commodity quotes. You can trade stocks on the system. Gateway to MCI Mail. It contains stock quotes, news, company profiles, financial analyses, and the full text of the *Wall Street Journal*.

NewsNet

NewsNet, Inc.

945 Haverford Road

Bryn Mawr, PA 19010

(800)345-1301 or (215)527-8030 in Pennsylvania.

Gives you access to the full text of more than 400 trade, industry, and investment newsletters, wire services, and TRW business profiles and credit reports.

NEXIS

Mead Data Central

9393 Springboro Pike

P.O. Box 933

Dayton, OH 45401

(800)227-4908

Contains complete text of hundreds of magazines, newspapers, wire services, and industry newsletters. Focus is on financial reports and medical information.

ORBIT Search Services

8000 Westpark Drive

McLean, VA 22101

(800)456-7248

Offers bibliographic citations and abstracts in over 100 individual databases. Main focus is on patents. Also provides technical and scientific information.

VU/TEXT

VU/TEXT Information Services, Inc.

325 Chestnut Street

Philadelphia, PA 19106

(800)258-8080

Offers the full text of over 70 metropolitan newspapers, stock quotes, and some bibliographic databases.

InfoMaster

1 Lake Street

Upper Saddle River, NJ 07458

(201)818-5000

Gives you access to databases from several vendors, including BRS, DIALOG, NewsNet, Orbit, and VU/TEXT.

Wilsonline

H.W. Wilson Company

950 University Avenue

Bronx, NY 10452

(800)367-6770

Offers online versions of the printed works, as the *Reader's Guide to Periodic Literature*, published by the H.W. Wilson Company.

Electronic Mail Services

Electronic mail services let you send messages to other PC users across the country and even, with some services, around the world. When you subscribe to an electronic mail service, you receive an electronic mailbox on a central computer. Other users of the electronic mail system can send messages to your mailbox, and you can send messages to them. You check for mail regularly, and you can copy messages that you want to keep to your PC.

AT&T Mail
AT&T Customer Assistance Center

P.O. Box 3505

New Brunswick, NJ 08903

(800)367-7225 ext 720

(800)624-5672

AT&T EasyLink
1 Lake Street
Upper Saddle River, NJ 07458
(800)527-5184
(800)624-5672

MCI Mail
MCI Communications Corporation
1111 19th St. NW, Fifth Floor
Washington, D.C. 20036
(800)444-6245 or (202)833-8484 in Washington, D.C.

INDEX

\>, 23
\\, 66, 71, 75
*, 76–77
:, 25
?, 76–77

A

A: drive, 7, 25–26
Accessories group window, 120–123
accounting programs, 14
active drive, 97
Active Task List window, 113–115
active window, changing, 135
adapters
  for added memory, 178
  for color graphics displays, 178
  for communications, 179–180
  for games, 178–179
  for monitors, 7, 178
  for plotters, 179
  for printers, 178
Alt key, 98, 151
Alt= key in WordPerfect, 151
Alt-Tab key in DOS 5 Shell, 113

application programs, 11–15, 141. *See also* Lotus 1-2-3; WordPerfect
  backing up, 142–143
  directories for, 67, 142, 143–144
  installing, 142
  loading, 143–144
  opening from Windows 3.0, 120–123
application windows, 120–123
arrow keys, 27–28
  in Lotus 1-2-3, 165, 168
  in WordPerfect, 151, 153
asterisk (*), 76–77
AT&T EasyLink, 214
AT&T Mail, 213

B

backing up, 197
  application programs, 142–143
  diskettes, 52–54, 197
  files, 145, 197. *See also* copying files
  hard disk, 83–87, 197
backslash (\\), 66, 71, 75
Backspace key, 21–22, 152, 154, 155

backup. *See* backing up; BACKUP command
BACKUP command, 84–86, 197
Bad command or file name message, 38
.BAS files, 74
.BAT files, 111
bits, 197
boot, 197
Break key, 42
BRS Information Technologies, 210
bugs, 198
Byte, 205–206
bytes, 198

C

C: drive, 7, 25–26
C prompt, 23
cancelling commands, 42
capital letters, 41
Caps Lock key, 41
Cardfile application, 130
   starting, 131–132
   working in, 132–134
case. *See* capital letters
cathode ray tubes, 7, 198
cell pointer in Lotus 1-2-3, 162, 165
cells in Lotus 1-2-3, 162
central processing unit, 3–4, 9, 198
changing
   active window, 135
   current drive, 25–26

directories (CHDIR), 69–70
directory tree display, 102–104
DOS 5 Shell display view, 99–101
CHDIR command, 69–70
checklists, 183–185
chips, 198
CHKDSK command, 59–61, 111
cleaning diskette drives, 61
clearing screen in WordPerfect, 159
colon (:), 25
color displays, 178
columns in Lotus 1-2-3, 161
.COM files, 111
commands, 37–38. *See also* DOS commands
   cancelling, 42
   Lotus 1-2-3, 167–168
   menus for, 43
   typing, 37–42
   using function keys for, 44, 150–152
   WordPerfect, 150–152
communications, 179–180, 208
complete backups, 83, 84–85
CompuServe, 209
Computer Shopper, 206
computers
   hardware components, 3–8
   optional equipment for, 175–180
   parts of, 3–15
   resetting, 30–31

Index

setting up, 189–195
software for, 10–15
turning on, 19–20
console, 7
control keys, 27. *See also* Ctrl key; Esc key
Control menu in Windows Program Manager, 120
control panel in Lotus 1-2-3, 162, 165
COPY command, 77–80, 83, 197
copying
    diskettes, 52–54, 142–143
    files in DOS 5 Shell, 108–109
    files to another directory, 79–80
    files to another disk, 77–79
    files to same directory, 80
    hard disk. *See* backing up hard disk
corrections, making, 21–22, 152
CPU, 3–4, 9, 198
crashes, 198
creating directories (MKDIR), 68–69
CRTs, 7, 198
Ctrl-Break key, 42
Ctrl key, 28–29, 151, 155
current date, setting, 20–21
current directory, 67, 69–70
current drive, 25–26, 67, 201
current time, setting, 20–21
cursor, 21
    keys for moving, 27–28
    in Lotus 1-2-3, 162
    in WordPerfect, 153
cursor, selection, 97

D

daisy wheel, 198–199
data, 199
Data-Star, 210–211
database vendors, 210–213
databases, 13–14, 199
date, setting, 20–21
date and time indicator in Lotus 1-2-3, 162
dBase, 14
debugging, 199
default drive, 25, 201
defaults, 199
DEL command, 81–83
Del key in WordPerfect, 154, 155
deleting. *See also* removing
    files, 81–83, 111
    text in WordPerfect, 154–156
Delphi, 209
density of diskettes, 48
desktop publishing, 14–15
DIALOG Information Services, 211
DIR command, 38–39, 40, 67, 68
directories, 65–66
    changing, 69–70
    creating, 68–69
    in DOS 5 Shell, 97, 101–104
    making, 68–69

naming, 67–68
removing, 72–73
directory tree, 97
   changing display of,
      102–104
   selecting directory from,
      101–102
disk drives. *See* diskette drives;
   hard disk
disk operating system. *See*
   DOS
Disk Utilities group (DOS 5
   Shell), 112–113
DISKCOPY command, 53–54,
   142–143, 197
diskette drives, 7
   additional, 176
   cleaning, 61
diskettes, 7, 47–48, 199
   backing up, 52–54,
      142–143, 197
   copying, 52–54, 197
   directories on, 65–66
   DOS 5 Shell utilities for,
      112–113
   formatting, 56–58
   handling, 49
   inserting, 23–24
   labeling, 50–51, 54
   listing files on, 38–39,
      100–101
   removing, 26
   reporting space on, 59–60
   saving files to, 145
   sizes of, 47
   space on, 58–61
   storing, 52
   types of, 47–48

   uses of, 7
   write-protecting, 55–56
disks. *See* diskettes
display adapters, 7, 178
displays, 7–8. *See also*
   monitors; screen display
   color, 178
   connecting, 192–193
   graphics, 178
.DOC files, 74
DOS, 10, 19, 95, 189
DOS 5 Shell, 10, 11, 96–98
   Active Task List window,
      113–115
   changing to drive A:
      using, 25
   changing view in, 99–101
   directory tree in, 101–104
   executing commands in,
      98–99
   file area in, 104–112
   File menu, 109, 110, 111
   Help menu, 98–99
   loading, 96
   Options menu, 104–105,
      113
   program area in, 112–113
   running executable files
      from, 111–112
   Tree menu, 103–104
   using mouse in, 98–99
   View menu, 99–101
DOS commands
   BACKUP, 84–86, 197
   CHDIR, 69–70
   CHKDSK, 59–61, 111
   COPY, 77–80, 83, 197
   DEL, 81–83

Index

DIR, 38–39, 40, 67, 68
DISKCOPY, 53–54, 142–143, 197
ERASE, 81–83
FORMAT, 57–58
MKDIR, 68–69
RENAME, 80
RESTORE, 86–87
RMDIR, 72–73
DOS prompt, 23
dot-matrix printers, 176, 177
double-density diskettes, 48
double-sided diskettes, 48
Dow Jones News/Retrieval Service, 211
downtime, 199
drive. *See also* diskette drives; hard disk drive
   active, 97
   current, 25–26
   default, 25
   displaying in DOS 5 Shell, 97
   in path names, 71–72

E

editing. *See* revising information
EGA display, 8
electronic mail, 179, 213–214
End key, 27, 155
enhanced keyboard, 5–6, 28
Enter key, 22–23
ERASE command, 81–83
erasing files, 81–83
error messages, 38, 76
Esc (escape) key, 29–30, 168
.EXE files, 111

exiting
   Lotus 1-2-3, 170–171
   WordPerfect, 159–160
expansion slots, 9–10
extensions for file names, 73–74

F

Family and Home Office Computing, 206
file area, DOS 5 Shell, 97, 104
   running executable files from, 111–112
   selecting files in, 107–108
File menu in DOS 5 Shell, 109, 110, 111
file names
   assigning, 73–77
   extensions for, 73–74
   rules for, 73–74
   system for, 74
   wild card characters in, 76–77
File not found message, 38, 76
files
   backing up, 145, 197. *See also* copying files
   copying, 77–80, 108–109, 197
   deleting, 81–83, 111
   DOS 5 Shell disk utilities for, 112–113
   erasing, 81–83
   listing, 38–39, 67, 68–69, 99–101
   manipulating in DOS 5 Shell, 108–112
   moving, 110–111

naming, 73–77
renaming, 80–81, 109–110
running from DOS 5 Shell, 111–112
selecting in DOS 5 Shell, 107–108
sorting in DOS 5 Shell, 104–106
filing systems
    backing up, 83–87
    designing, 65–67
    directories in, 68–73
    files in, 73
5 1/4 inch diskettes, 47, 48, 55, 56
fixed disk, 199. *See also* hard disk drive
floppy disk drives. *See* diskette drives
floppy disks, 199. *See also* diskettes
flowcharts, 200
FORMAT command, 57–58
formatting diskettes, 56–58, 112–113
formulas in Lotus 1-2-3, 167
freezing display, 39–40
function keys, 28, 29, 44, 151–152

G

games, 15, 178–179
GEnie, 209
gigabytes, 200
GoTo key in Lotus 1-2-3, 165
graphical interfaces
    DOS 5 Shell, 95
    Windows 3.0, 117–118
graphics, 14, 178

H

handling diskettes, 49
hard boot, 197
hard copy, 200
hard disk, 4–5
    backing up, 83–87
    directories on, 65–66
    installing DOS on, 19, 189
    operating without, 7
    reporting space on, 60–61
    saving files to, 144–145
    shutting down, 31
    storing files on, 145
hard disk drive, 4–5
hardware, 3–8, 14
heads, 200
Help menu in DOS 5 Shell, 98–99
high-density diskettes, 48
Home key, 27
Home Office Computing, 206

I

IBM keyboards, 5–6
incremental backups, 83, 85–86
InfoMaster, 213
information services, 208–214
InfoWorld, 206
input, 200
insert mode vs. typeover mode, 156–157

inserting
    diskettes, 23–24
    text in WordPerfect,
        153–154
installing
    application programs, 142
    DOS, 19, 189
interactive programs, 200
interfaces, 200

J

joystick, 178

K

keyboard, 5–6, 27–30
    adjusting, 194–195
    connecting, 191–192
    enhanced, 5–6, 28
    executing DOS 5 Shell
        commands with, 98, 99
    opening windows with,
        122–123
keypad, numeric, 27–28
keys. *See also names of keys*
    arrow, 27–28, 151, 153,
        165, 168
    cursor, 27–28, 153, 161
    function, 28, 29, 44,
        151–152
kilobytes, 59, 177, 200
kludge, 201

L

labeling diskettes, 50–51, 54
labels in Lotus 1-2-3, 164,
    165–166

laser printers, 176, 177, 201
leaving
    Lotus 1-2-3, 170–171
    WordPerfect, 159–160
letter-quality printers, 176, 177
line feed, 201
line printers, 201
lines of text, deleting, 154
listing files, 38–39, 67, 68–69,
    99–101
loading
    application programs,
        143–144
    DOS 5 Shell, 96
    Lotus 1-2-3, 161
    Windows 3.0, 118
    WordPerfect, 150–152
location for PCs, 190
logged drive, 25, 201
Lotus 1-2-3, 13, 160–161
    cell pointer in, 162, 165
    cells in, 162
    columns in, 161
    computer requirements
        for, 160
    control panel in, 162, 165
    creating reports in,
        164–167
    cursor in, 162
    date and time indicator
        in, 162
    exiting, 170–171
    loading, 161
    menus in, 167–168
    mode indicator in, 162
    printing files in, 169–170
    rows in, 161
    saving information in,
        169

screen in, 161-163
versions of, 160
worksheets in, 161-163
lowercase letters, 41

M

magazines, 205-208
making directories (MKDIR), 68-69
maximizing windows, 120, 128
MCI Mail, 214
Mead Data Central, 212
megabytes, 59, 177, 201
memory, 4, 59, 60, 144, 145, 201
  and 386 computers, 9
  additional, 177-178
menu bar
  in DOS 5 Shell, 97
  in Windows Program Manager, 120
menu pointer in Lotus 1-2-3, 168
menus, 43
  in DOS 5 Shell, 97
  in Lotus 1-2-3, 167-168
  in Windows 3.0, 123-124
  in WordPerfect, 151
messages. *See* error messages
microcomputers, 201
microprocessors, 198, 202
Microsoft Windows. *See* Windows 3.0
Minimize button (Windows Program Manager), 120
mistakes, correcting, 21-22, 152

MKDIR command, 68-69
mode indicator in Lotus 1-2-3, 162
modems, 179
monitors, 7-8
  adapter for, 7
  connecting, 192-193
monochrome graphics, 178
mouse, 8, 43, 202
  executing DOS 5 Shell commands with, 98-99
  opening windows with, 121-122
  in WordPerfect, 151, 155-156
moving files in DOS 5 Shell, 110-111
MS-DOS. *See* DOS

N

naming
  directories, 67-68
  files, 73-77
  subdirectories, 67-68
networks, 179, 202
NewsNet, 212
NEXIS, 212
Num Lock key, 27-28
numbers. *See* values
numeric keypad, 17-18

O

on-screen formatting, 12
1-2-3. *See* Lotus 1-2-3
Online Access, 206-207
online printing mode, 146

operating environment, 10–11, 202. *See also* DOS 5 Shell; Windows 3.0
operating systems. *See* DOS
optional equipment, 175–180
ORBIT Search Service, 212
output, 202

P

paging, 12
paper copy, 200
parameters, 38
path names, 70–72
    for files, 75–76
    in Lotus 1-2-3, 169
    shortcuts, 71–72
payroll programs, 14
PC Computing, 207
PC-DOS. *See* DOS
PC Magazine, 207
PC Week, 207
PC World, 207–208
PCs. *See* computers
PeaceNet, 156
peripherals, 202
PgDown key, 27
PgUp key, 27
.PIC files, 74
plotters, 179
power, on/off, 19–20, 31
power cord, connecting, 193–194
printers, 176–177
    daisy wheel, 198–199
    dot-matrix, 176, 177
    interface for, 200
    laser, 176, 177, 201

    letter-quality, 176, 177
    line, 201
printing, 146
    in Lotus 1-2-3, 169–170
    in WordPerfect, 158–159
problems, 183–185
program area, DOS 5 Shell, 97, 112–113
    Disk Utilities group, 112
    Main group, 112
Program Manager window, 119–120
programs, 4, 11–15
    running from DOS 5 Shell, 97
    switching between, 113–115
prompt (>), 23
public information services, 179, 208–209
Publish!, 208

Q

QBASIC, 112
question mark (?), 76–77

R

random access memory (RAM), 202
ranges in Lotus 1-2-3, 170
R:BASE, 14
read a disk, 203
read only memory (ROM), 203
removing. *See also* deleting
    directories (RMDIR), 72–73

diskettes, 26
RENAME command, 80
renaming files, 80–81, 109–110
resetting computers, 30–31
resizing windows, 127–128
response time, 203
RESTORE command, 86–87
restoring windows, 130–131
retrieving information, 145
Return key, 22
revising information, 145–146, 153–157
RF modulator, 8
RMDIR command, 72–73
ROM (read only memory), 203
root directory, 66
rows in Lotus 1-2-3, 161
rules
   for directory names, 67–68
   for file names, 73–74

S

saving files, 144–146
   in Lotus 1-2-3, 169
   in WordPerfect, 157, 159–160
   in Write application, 126
screen display. *See also* monitors
   clearing, in WordPerfect, 159
   in DOS 5 Shell, 96–98
   freezing, 39–40
   in Lotus 1-2-3, 161–163
   in Windows 3.0, 119–120
   in WordPerfect, 150

scroll bars, 97
scrolling, 12
   with mouse, 128–129
   stopping, 39–40
   using keyboard, 129
selection cursor, 97
service for PCs, 185–186
setting up PCs, 189–195
Shell. *See* DOS 5 Shell
Shift key, 25–26, 98, 151
silicon chips, 198
single-density diskettes, 48
single-sided diskettes, 48
sizes of diskettes, 48
slash (/) key, in Lotus 1-2-3, 168
soft boot, 197
software, 3, 10–15. *See also* application programs; operating environments
sorting files in DOS 5 Shell, 104–106
source diskette, 53
spreadsheets, 13, 160. *See also* Lotus 1-2-3
status line in DOS 5 Shell, 97
stopping display, 39–40
storage, 4, 58–61, 144–145
storing diskettes, 52
subdirectories, 66
Switch To command, 136
system unit, 3–4, 190–191

T

Tab key, 27, 98
target diskette, 53
task swapper, 113–115

Index 225

template for WordPerfect,
   151–152
terminals, 7–8
text
   deleting, 154–156
   entering, 152–157
   inserting, 153–154
   pasting, 136
3 1/2 inch diskettes, 47, 49–50,
   55, 57
386-class computers, 9
   and memory, 9
   running Windows 3.0 on,
     118
time, setting, 20–21
title bars
   DOS 5 Shell, 97
   Windows Program
     Manager, 120
Tree menu in DOS 5 Shell,
   103–104
troubleshooting, 183–185
turning on/off computers,
   19–20, 31
TV set as display, 8
typeover mode, 156–157

U

unpacking computers, 190–191
uppercase letters, 41
utilities, 112–113, 203. *See also*
   operating environments

V

values in Lotus 1-2-3, 164,
   166–167

VDTs, 7
VGA display, 8
video display terminals, 7
View menu in DOS 5 Shell,
   99–101
VU/TEXT, 212

W

wild card characters
   in file names, 76–77
   using to delete files, 82–83
WilsonLine, 214
window, active, 135
windows, 11, 203
   arranging, 132–134
   maximizing, 128
   multiple, 129–136
   opening, 131–132
   resizing, 127–128
   restoring, 130–131
   scrolling through,
     128–129
   transferring information
     among, 134–135
Windows 3.0, 10, 11, 117–118
   Accessories group
     window in, 120–123
   application windows in,
     120–123
   computer requirements
     for, 118
   loading, 118
   manipulating windows in,
     127–136
   Program Manager
     window in, 119–120
.WK1 files, 74

word processors, 12–13. *See also* WordPerfect; Write application
word wrapping in WordPerfect, 152, 154
WordPerfect, 12, 149–150
   arrow keys in, 151, 153
   clearing screen in, 159
   commands in, 150–152
   deleting text in, 154–156
   entering text in, 152–157
   exiting, 159–160
   function keys in, 151–152
   inserting text in, 153–154
   loading, 150–152
   printing files in, 158–159
   saving text in, 157, 159–160
   screen in, 150
   template in, 151–152
working directory, 69–70
worksheet in Lotus 1-2-3, 161–163
workspace (Windows Program Manager), 120
.WR1 files, 126
wrapping words in WordPerfect, 152, 154
Write application
   saving files in, 126
   using, 125–131
write-protecting diskettes, 55–56
writing to disk, 203

Selections from The SYBEX Library

OPERATING SYSTEMS

The ABC's of DOS 4
Alan R. Miller
275pp. Ref. 583-2

This step-by-step introduction to using DOS 4 is written especially for beginners. Filled with simple examples, *The ABC's of DOS 4* covers the basics of hardware, software, disks, the system editor EDLIN, DOS commands, and more.

ABC's of MS-DOS (Second Edition)
Alan R. Miller
233pp. Ref. 493-3

This handy guide to MS-DOS is all many PC users need to manage their computer files, organize floppy and hard disks, use EDLIN, and keep their computers organized. Additional information is given about utilities like Sidekick, and there is a DOS command and program summary. The second edition is fully updated for Version 3.3.

DOS Assembly Language Programming
Alan R. Miller
365pp. 487-9

This book covers PC-DOS through 3.3, and gives clear explanations of how to assemble, link, and debug 8086, 8088, 80286, and 80386 programs. The example assembly language routines are valuable for students and programmers alike.

DOS 3.3 On-Line Advisor Version 1.1
SYBAR, Software Division of SYBEX, Inc.
Ref. 933-1

The answer to all your DOS problems. The DOS On-Line Advisor is an on-screen reference that explains over 200 DOS error messages. 2300 other citations cover all you ever needed to know about DOS. The DOS On-Line Advisor pops up on top of your working program to give you quick, easy help when you need it, and disappears when you don't. Covers thru version 3.3. Software package comes with 3½" and 5¼" disks. **System Requirements:** IBM compatible with DOS 2.0 or higher, runs with Windows 3.0, uses 90K of RAM.

DOS Instant Reference SYBEX Prompter Series
Greg Harvey
Kay Yarborough Nelson
220pp. Ref. 477-1, 4 ¾" × 8"

A complete fingertip reference for fast, easy on-line help:command summaries, syntax, usage and error messages. Organized by function—system commands, file commands, disk management, directories, batch files, I/O, networking, programming, and more. Through Version 3.3.

Encyclopedia DOS
Judd Robbins
1030pp. Ref. 699-5

A comprehensive reference and user's guide to all versions of DOS through 4.0. Offers complete information on every

DOS command, with all possible switches and parameters—plus examples of effective usage. An invaluable tool.

Essential OS/2 (Second Edition)
Judd Robbins
445pp. Ref. 609-X

Written by an OS/2 expert, this is the guide to the powerful new resources of the OS/2 operating system standard edition 1.1 with presentation manager. Robbins introduces the standard edition, and details multitasking under OS/2, and the range of commands for installing, starting up, configuring, and running applications. For Version 1.1 Standard Edition.

Essential PC-DOS (Second Edition)
Myril Clement Shaw
Susan Soltis Shaw
332pp. Ref. 413-5

An authoritative guide to PC-DOS, including version 3.2. Designed to make experts out of beginners, it explores everything from disk management to batch file programming. Includes an 85-page command summary. Through Version 3.2.

Graphics Programming Under Windows
Brian Myers
Chris Doner
646pp. Ref. 448-8

Straightforward discussion, abundant examples, and a concise reference guide to graphics commands make this book a must for Windows programmers. Topics range from how Windows works to programming for business, animation, CAD, and desktop publishing. For Version 2.

Hard Disk Instant Reference
SYBEX Prompter Series
Judd Robbins
256pp. Ref. 587-5, 4 ¾" × 8"

Compact yet comprehensive, this pocket-sized reference presents the essential information on DOS commands used in managing directories and files, and in optimizing disk configuration. Includes a survey of third-party utility capabilities. Through DOS 4.0.

Inside DOS: A Programmer's Guide
Michael J. Young
490pp. Ref. 710-X

A collection of practical techniques (with source code listings) designed to help you take advantage of the rich resources intrinsic to MS-DOS machines. Designed for the experienced programmer with a basic understanding of C and 8086 assembly language, and DOS fundamentals.

Mastering DOS (Second Edition)
Judd Robbins
722pp. Ref. 555-7

"The most useful DOS book." This seven-part, in-depth tutorial addresses the needs of users at all levels. Topics range from running applications, to managing files and directories, configuring the system, batch file programming, and techniques for system developers. Through Version 4.

MS-DOS Power User's Guide, Volume I (Second Edition)
Jonathan Kamin
482pp. Ref. 473-9

A fully revised, expanded edition of our best-selling guide to high-performance DOS techniques and utilities—with details on Version 3.3. Configuration, I/O, directory structures, hard disks, RAM disks, batch file programming, the ANSI.SYS device driver, more. Through Version 3.3.

Understanding DOS 3.3
Judd Robbins
678pp. Ref. 648-0

This best selling, in-depth tutorial addresses the needs of users at all levels with many examples and hands-on exercises. Robbins discusses the fundamentals of DOS, then covers manipulating files and directories, using the DOS editor, printing, communicating, and finishes with a full section on batch files.

Understanding Hard Disk Management on the PC
Jonathan Kamin
500pp. Ref. 561-1

This title is a key productivity tool for all hard disk users who want efficient, error-free file management and organization. Includes details on the best ways to conserve hard disk space when using several memory-guzzling programs. Through DOS 4.

Up & Running with Your Hard Disk
Klaus M Rubsam
140pp. Ref. 666-9

A far-sighted, compact introduction to hard disk installation and basic DOS use. Perfect for PC users who want the practical essentials in the shortest possible time. In 20 basic steps, learn to choose your hard disk, work with accessories, back up data, use DOS utilities to save time, and more.

Up & Running with Windows 286/386
Gabriele Wentges
132pp. Ref. 691-X

This handy 20-step overview gives PC users all the essentials of using Windows—whether for evaluating the software, or getting a fast start. Each self-contained lesson takes just 15 minutes to one hour to complete.

WORD PROCESSING

The ABC's of Microsoft Word (Third Edition)
Alan R. Neibauer
461pp. Ref. 604-9

This is for the novice WORD user who wants to begin producing documents in the shortest time possible. Each chapter has short, easy-to-follow lessons for both keyboard and mouse, including all the basic editing, formatting and printing functions. Version 5.0.

The ABC's of WordPerfect
Alan R. Neibauer
239pp. Ref. 425-9

This basic introduction to WordPefect consists of short, step-by-step lessons—for new users who want to get going fast. Topics range from simple editing and formatting, to merging, sorting, macros, and more. Includes version 4.2

The ABC's of WordPerfect 5
Alan R. Neibauer
283pp. Ref. 504-2

This introduction explains the basics of desktop publishing with WordPerfect 5: editing, layout, formatting, printing, sorting, merging, and more. Readers are shown how to use WordPerfect 5's new features to produce great-looking reports.

The ABC's of WordPerfect 5.1
Alan R. Neibauer
352pp. Ref. 672-3

Neibauer's delightful writing style makes this clear tutorial an especially effective learning tool. Learn all about 5.1's new drop-down menus and mouse capabilities that reduce the tedious memorization of function keys.

The Complete Guide to MultiMate
Carol Holcomb Dreger
208pp. Ref. 229-9

This step-by-step tutorial is also an excellent reference guide to MultiMate features and uses. Topics include search/replace, library and merge functions, repagination, document defaults and more.

Encyclopedia WordPerfect 5.1
Greg Harvey
Kay Yarborough Nelson
1100pp. Ref. 676-6

This comprehensive, up-to-date WordPerfect reference is a must for beginning and experienced users alike. With complete, easy-to-find information on every WordPerfect feature and command—and it's organized by practical functions, with business users in mind.

FREE CATALOG!

SYBEX®

Mail us this form today, and we'll send you a full-color catalog of Sybex books.

Name _____
Street _____
City/State/Zip _____
Phone _____

Please supply the name of the Sybex book purchased.

_____

How would you rate it?

____ Excellent   ____ Very Good   ____ Average   ____ Poor

Why did you select this particular book?

____ Recommended to me by a friend
____ Recommended to me by store personnel
____ Saw an advertisement in _____
____ Author's reputation
____ Saw in Sybex catalog
____ Required textbook
____ Sybex reputation
____ Read book review in _____
____ In-store display
____ Other _____

Where did you buy it?

____ Bookstore
____ Computer Store or Software Store
____ Catalog (name: _____)
____ Direct from Sybex
____ Other: _____

Did you buy this book with your personal funds?

____ Yes   ____ No

About how many computer books do you buy each year?

____ 1-3   ____ 3-5   ____ 5-7   ____ 7-9   ____ 10+

About how many Sybex books do you own?

____ 1-3   ____ 3-5   ____ 5-7   ____ 7-9   ____ 10+

Please indicate your level of experience with the software covered in this book:

____ Beginner   ____ Intermediate   ____ Advanced

Which types of software packages do you use regularly?

_____ Accounting	_____ Databases	_____ Networks
_____ Amiga	_____ Desktop Publishing	_____ Operating Systems
_____ Apple/Mac	_____ File Utilities	_____ Spreadsheets
_____ CAD	_____ Money Management	_____ Word Processing
_____ Communications	_____ Languages	_____ Other _____

(please specify)

Which of the following best describes your job title?

_____ Administrative/Secretarial	_____ President/CEO
_____ Director	_____ Manager/Supervisor
_____ Engineer/Technician	_____ Other _____

(please specify)

Comments on the weaknesses/strengths of this book: _____

_____

_____

_____

_____

PLEASE FOLD, SEAL, AND MAIL TO SYBEX

SYBEX, INC.
Department M
2021 CHALLENGER DR.
ALAMEDA, CALIFORNIA USA
94501

SYBEX ®

SEAL

```
            SAM'S
            CLUB
    CLUB# 6320 HERMANTOWN MN

12/91 14:31 6320 6320 011        194

MBER 020901294 COLLECTOR'S CONNECT

 4945 BA-CYBEX ABC         11.47 T
       TAX DUE                 .75
       BALANCE DUE           12.22

       CASH                  52.29
       CHANGE DUE            40.00
           #ITEMS SOLD 1


SAVE AT S A M ' S  CLUB
```

WordPerfect 5.1

```
-




















                                                Doc 1 Pg 1 Ln 1" Pos 1"
```